Other People's Words

Other People's Words

The Cycle of Low Literacy

VICTORIA PURCELL-GATES

Harvard University Press
Cambridge, Massachusetts
London, England

Printed in the United States of America
Seventh printing, 2003

First Harvard University Press paperback edition, 1997

LIBRARY OF CONGRESS CATALOGING-IN-PUBLICATION DATA
Purcell-Gates, Victoria.
Other people's words : the cycle of low literacy / Victoria Purcell-Gates.
p. cm.
Includes bibliographical references and index.
ISBN 0-674-64497-2 (cloth)
ISBN 0-674-64511-1 (pbk.)
1. Literacy—Social aspects—Appalachian Region, Southern—Case studies. 2. Socially handicapped—Education—Appalachian Region, Southern—Case studies. 3. Educational anthropology—Appalachian Region, Southern—Case studies. I. Title.
LC152.A66P87 1995
302.2'244'0974—dc20 94-31073
CIP

To "Jenny"

Contents

Acknowledgments

I wish to express my deepest appreciation to the many people who have supported my efforts to record Jenny and Donny's story. Above all, Jenny's willingness to share her struggles and goals with me made this book possible. I will always treasure her humor, honesty, and outrage. The two years we spent together changed me as a person and as a professional; I am eternally grateful.

This work was also supported financially at different times through small grants from both the College of Education at the University of Cincinnati and the Harvard Graduate School of Education. Part of this money allowed me to employ the transcription services of Sue McGrath, who provided wonderfully accurate records of my meetings with Jenny and Donny both in the Literacy Lab and at their home.

Emotional and intellectual support for this work came primarily from my best friend, mentor, and husband, Joel Milgram, who listened to me for hours as I related my experiences with Jenny and Donny and worked out my evolving interpretations. He provided a keen ear and gave me invaluable advice over the course of the project. His willingness to read through draft after draft of the manuscript is greatly appreciated.

I also wish to thank my colleagues Lilia Bartolomé and Marjorie Roemer, who gave up their valuable time to read and comment on the first draft. The book is better and stronger for their efforts. And I wish to thank Penny Freppon for maintaining contact with Jenny and her family, continuing their literacy education, and providing me with follow-up samples of their work.

Finally, I am grateful to the National Endowment for the Humanities for the 1993 Summer Stipend Award that allowed me the luxury of focusing full time on the book for several months.

A portion of Chapter 5 was published in an earlier form in the *Journal of Reading,* 37 (1993): 210–219, under the title "I Ain't Never Read My *Own* Words Before." In addition, a summary of parts of the study is presented in the chapter "Nonliterate Homes and Emergent Literacy," in *Children's Emergent Literacy,* edited by D. E. Lancy (Westport, Conn.: Praeger). With the exception of my own, the names of all people, neighborhoods, and towns have been changed to protect the privacy of all involved.

Other People's Words

Introduction: Literacy, Schools, and Society

Jenny was poor, of a low-caste group, and, when I met her, virtually nonliterate. Donny, her son, was unable to read anything beyond his name, although he had just been promoted to second grade. They were both products of the public school system of the United States of America—a system that has provided more education for more of its citizens than any other country in the world. Yet in the generations since we first promised access to education for all of our citizens, the problem of low literacy among children from the nation's poor populations has proved intractable. Jenny's and Donny's stories are among the many that haunt us.

Over time, educators and researchers have struggled with this apparent failure of our schools. Recently, interest in the problem has increased as news of our falling status internationally has again shocked us with evidence that all is not as it should be. When we look at the data, we must acknowledge that the poor, minority, and most often urban children fall significantly behind their middle-class counterparts in their ability to read and write. These children have, over the generations, grown up to be non- or low-literate adults and parents of future generations of struggling children.

Jenny and her family represent those with whom educators are most concerned. When we began to work together, neither she nor her husband could read beyond a few isolated words. Neither could write except to sign their names. Jenny reported that many of their friends and neighbors were also unable to read or write. Jenny and Big Donny, her husband, had two children: Donny, a second grader, and Timmy, who was four years old when I first met the family. Donny was well on his way to repeating the failure experienced by his parents. Timmy's prospects looked equally dim. Jenny and her family belong to the white underclass, a minority within the nation's white majority and a population that has received relatively little attention from researchers or policymakers. The discrimination and stereotyping they face from mainstream communities is not as visible as for minority people of color, but the effects are just as insidious and as costly to society.

For two years I worked with Jenny and Donny as a teacher, a guide, a mentor, and a friend. With their permission, I recorded most of our transactions, took field notes, and saved artifacts. I offered them my time and talents as a teacher, and they offered me their insights into the difficult process of learning to read and write. My research and tutoring took me increasingly into their home and their lives. We established a close personal relationship over time, with a deep mutual respect and affection that continue to this day. Although I have moved from their city, we correspond by letter and, occasionally, talk on the phone.

Theoretical Lens

Efforts to explain the overall failure of low socioeconomic status minority populations to attain literacy levels commensurate with the middle class have fallen short, and closing the achievement gap has proved elusive. For years, professionals and public opinion have held on to the notion that poor and minority peoples are deficient in important ways. The list of supposed deficiencies is long and inclusive: deficient cognitive abilities, deficient language, poor motivation, devaluation of education, poor parenting skills. To a large degree these attitudes and beliefs about this segment of the population persist. *''Those people''* don't care about education, or are genetically unfit, or cannot even speak correctly, much less learn to read and write standard English. From the level of policymaking to the individual classroom, such deficit-ridden views of children who come from poor and minority homes continue to have an impact on the education to which they are exposed.

Sociocultural View of Learning

Deficit explanations, however, are being replaced within research and theoretical circles with one that views all learners from a sociocultural theory of learning. This shift in perspective has come about as a result of accumulating evidence that all communities have appropriate cognitive abilities, albeit different ones to fit varied life situations. Similarly, language variation between groups reflects community use and norms, resulting in dialects and registers that must be judged not relative to some "perfect" language but rather to their effectiveness in varying contexts. In addition, the growing influence of educational research grounded in anthropological perspectives has eroded the ethnocentric stance responsible for deficit explanations. We can no longer make judgments about the abilities and/or disabilities of peoples from sociocultural groups different from our own, using "our" group as the standard (no matter which group is "ours"). Those judgments are seen by an ever-growing segment of the research field as invalid, unhelpful, and destructive.

It was through the lens of this sociocultural theory of learning that I conducted the research reported in this book. From this perspective, all learners are seen as members of a defined culture, and their identity with this culture determines what they will encode about the world and the ways in which they will interpret information.

The insight that everyone processes information

through a cultural lens is crucial to any attempt to explore the processes by which some learners predictably succeed in our schools and others, equally predictably, fail. Many cultures are represented in the classrooms of today, including mainstream, majority ones. Members of these varied cultural groups, including the teachers, the curriculum designers, and the children, are not perceiving the schooling experience in identical ways. They are in many ways living in different worlds, though ostensibly engaging in the same activity—schooling—in the same place—the classroom.

Socioeconomic status, religion, family education history, gender, ethnicity, sociopolitical status—all of these sociocultural factors intertwine and interact to result in individual cultural identities. A Hispanic female child from a low socioeconomic status home whose parents are high school dropouts will perceive the world differently from a male Hispanic child from a low socioeconomic status home whose parents are high school dropouts. Similarly, a female Anglo child from a low socioeconomic status home whose parents are high school dropouts will perceive the world differently from a female Anglo child from a middle-class home whose parents are college graduates. And so on. Any permutation of the critical sociocultural descriptors will reflect a shift in cultural identity.[1] Thus when we seek to understand learners, we must seek to understand the cultural contexts within which they have developed, learned to interpret who they are in relation to others, and learned how to process, interpret, or decode, their world.

The sociocultural theory of learning also suggests that all learning takes place within a social context, and to understand the processes of learning, one must also specify and seek to understand the social context within which learning occurs. To understand and gain useful insights into literacy learning, one must thus explore the classroom settings and other settings within which people learn to read and write. This exploration includes describing how literacy is defined in each setting, what counts as literacy knowledge, who gets to participate in events, and how this participation is defined.[2] The goal is to understand how the participants perceive, interpret, and evaluate what they are doing.

It is this sociocultural theoretical lens, I believe, that offers us the best chance of understanding the low literacy attainment by poor and minority peoples. How can we understand *why* so many children do not learn what the mainstream schools think they are teaching unless we can get "inside" the learners and see the world through their eyes? If we do not try to do this, if we continue to use the mainstream experience of reality as the perspective, we fool ourselves into believing that we are looking through a window when instead we are looking into a mirror. Our explanations threaten to reflect only ourselves and our world, serving no real explanatory purpose.

Emergent Literacy

Jenny's experience speaks not only to issues of sociocultural research but to the field of emergent literacy.

Research in this area has, over the past fifteen to twenty years, documented what and how children learn about reading and writing in their homes and communities during the pre-formal instruction years. The term *emergent literacy* reflects the theoretical underpinning of this research: that literate abilities and stances emerge developmentally as children observe and engage in experiences mediated by print in their daily lives. This perspective is seen as different from the traditional view that children *begin* to learn to read and write only at the onset of formal literacy instruction.[3]

While some emergent literacy researchers have focused on mapping the details of emerging skills, attitudes, and behaviors associated with literacy, others have sought to understand the interplay between what has been learned before beginning school and how literacy learning proceeds within the classroom. As one of the latter group of researchers, my initial question, upon listening to Jenny, was, How *could* Donny and Timmy learn to read and write when neither of their parents did? What roles, if any, did his parents' nonliteracy have to play in Donny's difficulties in school?

I understood these questions initially as purely cognitive ones. I was thinking of schema: with no prior experiences in the home with print, how did Donny "make sense of" the instruction in school, which focused on letters, sounds, words—reading and writing. Over time, I came to see the ways in which literacy and nonliteracy were cultures. More specifically, I moved to a view of cognition as culture-bound. I came to see Jenny and Donny's nonliteracy as a cultural influence, one that had a significant impact upon their strategies for "making sense" of literacy instruction.

Although my initial research focus was on the relationship between the nonliteracy in Donny's home and his difficulty in learning to read and write in school, I soon realized that this focus must expand to include the family's membership in a low-caste minority group known as urban Appalachian. The close interrelationships between the family's failure to acquire functional literacy skills and their status in the urban society surfaced early in the research and became another lens through which to interpret the data.

As I proceeded, I placed Jenny and Donny within two primary cultural communities, or contexts. One context was the nonliteracy of their home, and thus I sought to determine how the world looked through the eyes of a nonliterate. Another context was their membership in the community of urban Appalachians.What does the world look like from this perspective? In addition, as we shall see, Jenny's identity as an urban Appalachian woman and Donny's as a young urban Appalachian man affected their beliefs toward, motivations for, and eventual successes with literacy. Ultimately, I sought to determine the dynamic relationship resulting from the confluence of these nested cultural contexts: what does the world look like through the eyes of a nonliterate, gendered, urban Appalachian?[4]

The resulting account of Jenny and Donny's experience provides a graphic picture of the myriad ways in which social, cultural, and cognitive factors influence the degree to which our schools, as they are configured today, are successful in transmitting literacy knowledge to children in a culturally diverse society. A chilling picture also emerges of the ways in which certain Discourses—forms of life or "ways of being," according to James Gee,[5] "which integrate words, acts, values, beliefs, attitudes, and social identities"—serve to admit only the favored few to the fruits of education and block access for others.

At the same time, I believe that Jenny's story is an account of one woman's courage and persistence. In attempting to break through the wall of illiteracy and prejudice, she sought to ensure a better future for her children. Her sense of self and her determination to move forward in the face of great odds have much to teach all of us.

1

Nonliterate in an American City

This is the story of Jenny and Donny, a mother and son who are trying to learn to read and write. They live in a midwestern city in the United States of America. The city is relatively prosperous, and so are many of its residents. A major state university is situated there.

This city is not known for its crime rate or for its poor schools. In fact, it rather prides itself on its "hometown" flavor; it is commonly said that it is a great place to raise children with traditional American values. The majority of its residents were born there, grew up in one of its many neighborhoods, and intend to live and work, raise their children, and die there. Over the years, the population has spread outward to create suburban neighborhoods and townships, but never at the cost seen in other big cities. The city, itself, still includes prosperous and professional families as well as working class ones. During the year, traditional "festivals" bring the suburban residents into the city center to celebrate with their city-dwelling neighbors. People from outlying rural areas and smaller towns regularly trek into the city to shop in its many "upscale" department stores or to sample one of the many cultural activities sponsored by the city: the opera, the symphony, the theater, and the ballet.

Jenny and Donny, however, have never been to an opera or a ballet. Nor have they ever shopped in one of the upscale stores. They never travel the mile of city blocks from their home to the downtown area where these establishments can be found. There are many reasons for this, but one is that no one in the family can read well enough to use the bus line that could take them there. They could drive one of their several cars, but no one in the family can read well enough to read the street signs or store names. They can, and do, use familiar landmarks to travel by car to some locations in the city—the welfare office, the grocery store, and the veterinarian's. Mainly, they drive out of town whenever they can, along interstates, with their numbered exits, and familiar backroads.

There is, of course, an urban poor population in this city as in all cities. It is largely made up of two ethnic minorities—African Americans and urban Appalachians, blacks and whites. Jenny and Donny are urban Appalachian. They and Big Donny and Timmy live in the central city, for the most part segregated from their African American peers. They do not live in the worst of the ghettos, a twelve-square-block nest of grinding poverty, crime, sickness, and despair. Rather, they live at the bottom of the hill upon which the university reigns, just across the interstate that separates them from densely populated Camp Fairwell, the urban Appalachian ghetto in which Jenny grew up and where her brother and other relatives still live. Camp Fairwell is close enough for her to walk—under the overpass and she's there in twenty minutes—to use the phone when hers is cut off and the family's cars are inoperable.

Donny attends one of the city schools, just as his mother and father did before him. The school is integrated, with both African American and urban Appalachian children. He had attended one year of Head Start, at another location, and then one year of first grade. Kindergarten is not required in this city, although most children do attend. Donny did not, however, because Jenny did not know about it. Because she cannot read, she has to rely on friends to tell her about things like this, and no one told her about kindergarten.

At the beginning of his second-grade year, Donny could not read or write anything but his first name and, occasionally when prompted, the word *the.* When asked to read a nearly memorized text, he runs his finger under whole lines of print while "reading" one or two words. He is still unsure about one-third of the letters in the alphabet, reverses his b's and d's, and has such an aversion to reading that he will cover his eyes and exclaim, "No, no! No words for me!"

Aside from this, he is a bright, mischievous, artistically talented young boy. Polite and deferential, he is filled with ideas and his eyes gleam with humor. He loves to make things and can utilize any material—paper, string, wood, glue, glitter—in his spontaneous creations. He also loves stories, both oral ones and those read to him from books. He adores his father, loves his mother, and is careful to take care of his brother Timmy, as a big brother must. He speaks with a soft Appalachian drawl and draws upon this lively dialect to enhance his many recollections and stories.

Jenny dropped out of school in the seventh grade—as did Big Donny, after repeating it three times. She reports that neither she nor Big Donny "can read a lick." About half of their friends, relatives, and neighbors are also unable to read, according to her. She wants to learn to read well enough to be able to help Donny with his school work. She knows he cannot read any words and is angry that the school passed him on to second grade. She is frustrated that he brings home homework which he cannot do and with which she cannot help him. The five spelling words Donny's teacher sends home each week with a different activity each day ("arrange alphabetically," "put each word in a sentence," and so on) are beyond her. The list contains words like *bug* and *sun*. Not only can she not read the spelling words; she cannot read the directions from the teacher—"arrange alphabetically"—and Donny seems unable to help. Although she has "plainly told" the teacher that neither she nor Big Donny can read, the school continues to send written work home and to penalize Donny for not doing it or for doing it incorrectly. Eventually Jenny found her way up the hill to the university where I work.

"They ain't gonna do my kid like they done me and

his dad!" she protested. "They know he can't read, but they're just gonna pass him on. That don't do no good; I know!"

Thus I first met Jenny in my office at the university. Long straight brownish blond hair hung lankly to her shoulders, and her faded blue eyes looked straight at me with determination. Jenny told me that while Big Donny preferred to accept his nonliteracy, she wanted to learn to read and had begun attending a neighborhood-based adult education center. She wanted to be able to read children's books to her kids. She also wanted to be able to shop in new places without asking friends to come along to read labels and signs for her.

"It's hard not knowin' how to read. Some people think it's easy . . . just sit down and do it. But it ain't."

Jenny was particularly concerned about the effect of her nonliteracy on Donny's ability to learn to read and write in school. This drove her to find her way to the university-based Literacy Center, which I directed, to seek help. She knew that the Center only served children in grades 1–12, but she asked if there was any way she could "sit alongside" her son as we taught him. I suggested the following arrangement: I would work with Donny and her personally (graduate students were the primary teachers in the Center). In return, I asked her permission to record our work together so that I might study how she and her son learned to read and write. She agreed, and we began our two-year association.

Although I had devoted over twenty years to helping children and adults who have experienced problems learning to read and write, I had never before encountered a totally nonliterate family. Indeed all of my training, experience, and research led me to question Jenny's assertion that neither she nor Big Donny could read a lick. I suspected that they could read something, even if it was not school related. If it did turn out, though, that Donny and Timmy were growing up in a nonliterate home, the implications of this for their own learning were immense. How could this happen in the United States today? What were and are the schools doing with their Jennys and Donnys? What can we learn from this case?

2

Jenny and Donny's World

Jenny and her family are members of a low-status minority group that makes up a significant proportion of poor urban dwellers throughout the Midwest and scattered cities elsewhere.[1] The members of this group are known as "urban Appalachians," a name that reflects their common heritage and history: people from the Appalachian mountain regions who have migrated to the cities in search of work and a better life for their children.

Urban Appalachians: The "Invisible Minority"

Urban Appalachians have been called the "invisible minority," a term that reflects both the general lack of knowledge about them outside of the cities in which they reside and the fact that they are overwhelmingly white and thus are not recognized as a minority in a political climate that equates "minority" with "people of color." Two scholars who study urban Appalachians, Phillip Obermiller and Michael Maloney, write that they are "invisible because their culture is not recognized and minority because when it is recognized, it is not accepted by individuals and institutions in the urban mainstream."[2]

That urban Appalachians qualify as an ethnic group or as a cultural entity is not universally agreed upon, even among scholars.[3] There is clear consensus, however, that they constitute a recognizable group set apart by culture and values that they brought with them to the cities and retained through kin networks and separate neighborhoods. Obermiller and Maloney provide a descriptive synthesis of urban Appalachians:

> . . . this group is predominantly white, mostly Baptist or Pentecostal, and heavily blue-collar. They are for the most part of Scots-Irish or Anglo-Saxon heritage, speak with a distinct accent, and enjoy country and western, bluegrass, and "old time" gospel music. . . . Appalachian neighborhoods [are] replete with "hillbilly" bars and restaurants, Pentecostal and Baptist churches, and people speaking with mountaineer accents. Other typical lifestyle features of blue-collar Appalachian neighborhoods include pickup trucks equipped with hunting rifles, campers, body shops, and shade-tree mechanics working on their vehicles.[4]

During the mid-twentieth century, following the failure of family farms and the closing of the coal mines, migration from rural mountain areas into metropolitan ones was heavy and carried significant implications both for the southern regions left behind and for the cities that received the newcomers. Many of the Appalachian migrants acquired jobs that permitted them to improve the economic well-being of their children and to move into working-class or middle-class neighborhoods and out of the central city cores. Small towns that surround the metropolitan core cities also became heavily populated by migrants from Appalachia.[5] Many of the men took jobs in tire factories, automobile plants, or as construction workers. Some Appalachian women became teachers, nurses, and social workers. Others took jobs in food processing or toy assembly plants.[6]

A portion of the migrants, though, never succeeded in assimilating into urban or suburban society. They live a marginal existence, eking out a living with nonskilled labor and yearning to return to their mountain homes. Jenny and her family are members of this group. It is this subgroup of the Appalachian migrant population on which I will focus and refer to as urban Appalachian.[7]

Jenny's family left their farm in eastern Kentucky when she was three years old. They moved to the city to get medical treatment for one of her older brothers, who suffered from a liver ailment.

"My dad had to sell the farm and his land and stuff to my Uncle Bob in order to move up here to take Robert to these hospitals," she recalls.

Once in the city, they moved in with relatives until they could find a place of their own. Her brother died of his illness within two years, but it was too late to move back.

Appalachian migrants usually move into voluntarily segregated neighborhoods in the cities. The predominant social organization system of this population is the family-kinship relation. Thus when individual family units migrate, the initial destinations are usually the homes of kin in specific city neighborhoods. Large family networks can be found within single neighborhoods, and everyday life usually involves relatives in and out of each other's homes.[8] These neighborhoods are for the most part complete, with churches, food and clothing stores, drug stores, bars, and restaurants.

Jenny and her two remaining brothers and two sisters grew up in one of these urban Appalachian "ghettos" (her term), one of several that exist in this city. Here they were surrounded by relatives and friends, all of whom lived in comparable poverty. Jenny remembers those years fondly, where life consisted of tightly knit groups of children playing among the abandoned and run-down buildings during the week and, if money was available, returning to their mountain homes on the weekends.

Life was hard, though, and often unpleasant. Cultural alienation, poverty, and breakdowns in familial and societal networks have contributed to the ills of urban Appalachian families. Obermiller describes the social conditions:

> Urban Appalachians in poverty have high rates of coronary heart disease, diabetes, and work-related

> disabilities. Their children suffer from lack of perinatal care, poor nutrition, and the effects of urban pollution. Sexually transmitted diseases affect many Appalachian teenagers. Among all generations of urban Appalachians, injuries related to work are common as are illnesses due to stress and diet such as diabetes, hypertension, and heart disease.[9]

Jenny describes her dad as a "drunk" and her mom as someone who worked during the day and drank at night and on the weekends.

"After we moved up here, then Mommy got to workin', and when Daddy was workin' at [a factory], got some kind of steel or somethin' in his eye. He couldn't see that good so he got fired or quit from there or somethin'. Then he worked somewhere else and quit. Then he was workin' with his brothers, you know, tree work and paintin' an' stuff."

Her father worked sporadically in this manner until he died of a heart attack in his fifties. Jenny's mother worked in a store and sold beauty products on the side. A heavy smoker, she died the year after I worked with Jenny of pneumonia, a recurrent illness. Jenny also contracts pneumonia regularly and is "laid up" by it at least twice a year. Each occurrence is more severe and lasts longer. She knows she should quit smoking, but so far she cannot go more than two or three days without a cigarette.

Harsh tragedy stalked Jenny's family as it so often seems to afflict other urban Appalachians. Soon after we met, one of Big Donny's brothers, visiting back in the mountains, died in a trailer fire when a gasoline container burst into flames. One of Jenny's sisters was shot in the head by her husband and suffers periodic physical and mental after-effects. Jenny's sister-in-law, distraught over the death of her husband in the trailer fire, turned to alcohol and increasingly ignored her three children. They were soon wandering the streets during school hours, dirty and hungry. Jenny took them in and cared for them when she could, but put her foot down and refused to have them in her house when they all became infested with head lice and their mother refused to treat it. The oldest of these children became pregnant at fourteen and appealed to Jenny to intercede with her mother so that she could be seen at the local health clinic.

Goin' Down Home

The urban Appalachian's enduring tie to "down home" was illustrated for me soon after I met Jenny and Donny. Urban Appalachian migrants to the cities and their descendants frequently return home for visits and occasional resettlement. Return visits reflect not only nostalgia for mountain life but also real attempts to maintain family relationships.[10] Jenny's family was no exception. Visits down home for Jenny and her family took three to four hours by car.

In the context of reassuring me that she always saw to it that Donny attended school regularly, Jenny told me one day about taking her dog home for burial.

"See, I don't let him [Donny] miss. He's been to school ever' day this year—except when Brindi died.

We all loved that dog and when he died, we had to take him down home to be buried. That took about two days 'cause of the rain that kept us from burying him right when we got there."

Over our two-year association, Jenny transported several animals home for burial, once driving down and back overnight with a friend, the kids asleep in the back seat, to ensure that Donny did not miss school and that she did not miss her once-a-week job cleaning house for a family in the suburbs. When Jenny's mother died, the mortuary drove her body down home for the funeral and burial in the family plot. All members of Jenny's and Big Donny's families have been, and will be, buried down home with the rest of their people.

The family went home as often as possible on weekends. Only the lack of money could keep them in the city. At times, Donny would be allowed to go down with relatives or friends, many of whom could be found making the trip on any given weekend. During the summer and school vacations, he would be allowed to stay over a week or two with relatives who still lived on the ancestral land.

These visits down home were favorite times for all members of the family. Although Jenny had been only three years old when her family migrated, she retained a strong sense of the mountains as home. Donny and Timmy had absorbed this and, in concert with their frequent visits "home," indicated through their tales and stories that they much preferred the life down home over that offered by the city. Roscoe Giffin, an

Appalachian researcher, contrasts city life over mountain life from the child's perspective: "Children who accompany parents to the city find themselves in a world which denies them many, if not most, of the sources of satisfaction which they knew in the hills. In place of woods, they are given the sidewalk, a small unkempt courtyard, a noisy, dangerous street and an occasional city recreation center with a wading pool and cemented playground."[11]

Jenny loved the fact that, down home, the kids could be set out to play in the woods and hollers with little fear for their safety. "Four-wheeler" vehicle riding was a favorite sport when they were down home, and Jenny and Donny both regaled me with stories of the hours of fun experienced out of the city. Jenny's abiding fear of snakes entered into the following vignette:

> We'd drive the cars just so far, and then, you know, they [the husbands and other men in their group] had to come up out o' the woods for to get us. And we was goin' down [in a four-wheeler], and the kids and Big Donny was already down in there. Me and the girls and us was goin' down. Was me, Charles, Peggy, and Peggy's little grandbaby, Earl, Little Earl's sister on one, Dina, Rayna on another one. We was goin' down, and there was a rattlesnake! You know, we didn't get to it right then. The others, they was flyin' away, goofin' off, but Charles didn't 'cause we had the baby on with us. And they kept motionin' for us to back up, and Charles said "What for?" He looks like Matt Dillon; he's got a big ol' mustache;

> he's got a gun here (indicates the hip) and a knife here (the other hip). (Laughing) And they said, "A rattlesnake!" And so Charles said, "Where?" It was right beside the bank! So he's tryin' to run up over it. And it got up on the bank away from him. And he was hollerin' for 'em to git him somethin' and kill it with. And Maggie—that's his wife—she was behind him. She smacked him, and she said "Kill it! Shoot it with your gun, stupid!" So he got it. You know, we's not this far away from it! And anyway, he was shootin' at it, but it got away. I love it, you know, goin' jeep ridin' and four-wheelin'!

Jenny's family talked often about moving "back home." At regular intervals, various items of furniture, dishes, and toys would be transported south in anticipation of this move. The adults would ponder employment possibilities, which were dim, and plan their housing arrangements. Donny and Timmy gleefully looked forward to the day when they would move back home and fantasized about how their lives would be different. They envisioned themselves playing in the woods, four-wheeling, doing farm chores, and (according to Donny) missing school on a permanent basis due to all of these activities. To the children, the move home was real and imminent. To Jenny and Big Donny it was a hopeful vision, something to look forward to when city life was especially hard, which was often.

Prejudice and Stereotype

Urban Appalachians are heavily stereotyped by people from mainstream cultures. They are the objects of perhaps the last socially acceptable ethnic and social prejudice in this country. They are the butt of ethnic jokes and are portrayed in negative and stereotyped ways in movies *(Deliverance)*, on television *(Beverly Hillbillies)*, and in comic strips (*L'il Abner* and *Snuffy Smith*). Their predilection for returning down home for visits is often the subject of "hillbilly" jokes. The scholars C. B. McCoy and V. M. Watkins provide the following example:

> When St. Peter was showing some visitors through heaven, he was showing off the lavishly furnished rooms and the excellent attention given to all the people. Of course, the visitors were very impressed by the heavenly living arrangements of all the people until they came upon the Ohio room where they were astonished to find that about half the people were tied up and not permitted to move. St. Peter assured the visitors that this was not normal, but this was the weekend, and if these Kentucky hillbillies were not tied up, they would leave heaven and go back to Kentucky.[12]

"Hillbillies," "ridgerunners," and "briarhoppers" are among the pejorative terms used to refer to urban Appalachians like Jenny and her family. Prevalent stereotypes include ignorance, laziness, uncleanliness, and immorality:

> Why was Jesus Christ not born in Kentucky? God replies that he had searched diligently in Kentucky but could not find three wise men nor a virgin.[13]

> "Did you know that the old country preacher was arrested?" "No." "Yes, he was arrested for polluting

the Ohio River." "How did that happen?" "He was baptizing hillbillies in the river."[14]

Scholars point out that, while African American migrants are discriminated against in part because of their color, Appalachian migrants are discriminated against because of cultural differences between mountain subculture and urban culture. These differences extend to mannerisms, customs, and, in particular, speech patterns.[15]

Jenny was quite aware of the impact her speech had on her lack of success in school. "[I couldn't learn to read] . . . 'cause I talk different. 'Cause I'm you know . . . countrified, and my words don't come out the way they're suppose to. That's the way I was brought up!"

Along with their language, migrants from Appalachia brought with them characteristic traits and customs that, though changed and shaped by interactions with city life, can still be recognized. Heavy reliance on family networks—rather than social agencies—to find employment or to provide temporary housing is one example of this. Seeking public assistance in the form of charity or welfare is considered to be a step of last resort by those without family support.[16]

Jenny's clear reluctance to accept charity from an outsider was a reflection of the traditional Appalachian trait of independence. She refused to accept paper, pencils, and crayons from me when I suggested that she provide access to these items for Donny at home. Although she didn't have the money to purchase them in the city, she knew she could obtain them cheaply at the Dollar Store down home. Within two weeks, she had done this.

Perhaps the most vivid example of her insistence on "paying her way" was her reaction to my providing instruction for Donny in exchange for her permission to record and write about the experience as research. No matter how many times I tried to explain "research," my impression was that she did not really believe that this was a valuable item—at least not equal to instruction in reading and writing. Too polite to say so, she proceeded to pay me in her own way. Over time, she collected enough fabric scraps from the dumpster outside the shirt mill down home and in the evenings put together a beautiful, colorful quilt. She presented this to me as a "Thank You" and continued to look for other ways to pay me. Over the two years I received clothing, given to Jenny by the women whose houses she cleaned, and items of food—all of which I greatly appreciated.

An emphasis on self-sufficiency is also apparent in the general ability of urban Appalachian families to cope with day-to-day needs. Skilled in a number of ways many middle-class families are not, the urban Appalachian takes care of mechanical breakdowns, plumbing problems, and general home maintenance without outside assistance. My relative helplessness became increasingly apparent to me as I observed Jenny, Big Donny, and a host of relatives repair each other's cars, using parts garnered from a collection of old vehicles kept in each other's yards and garages. In situations that would force me to call a repair person, they would either do the work themselves or call a relative. Jenny, who regularly repainted her house inside and out, politely scoffed at the inability of the "rich and educated" to take care of themselves in this way.

Scholars have speculated that another cultural tradition brought to the city is the southern mountain people's criteria of success.[17] A strong tendency to accept one's environment as is rather than trying to master it may, they suggest, translate in the city to a resistance to urban goals and standards of achievement and a reluctance to pursue a level of consumption and employment that others regard as desirable.

Jenny told me that she felt no desire for wealth or upward mobility. Her only needs were enough money to pay the bills, buy food to eat, and have enough left over for fun like "four-wheelin' " on the weekends. She felt sorry for some of the women she worked for who shared with her their worries about being robbed or losing their money to greedy relatives. She didn't want the "headaches" that she believed wealth would bring.

Related to independence of spirit and existence is the trait of straight-talking. The mountaineer's way of saying what has to be said as simply and straightforwardly as possible is part of our lore. It is also a trait supposedly held by the early westerners and others who live relatively unsophisticated lives.

Jenny's way of expressing herself was refreshingly clear and unambiguous. She spoke honestly, directly, and with sensitivity at all times, often in direct contrast to those fellow urban dwellers who made up the bureaucracy against which she struggled. Jenny's and Donny's social sensitivity showed up in their avoidance of certain topics or statements, and never in prevarication or "double talk." Jenny found it nearly impossible to comprehend why the people at Donny's school failed to understand her. She had gone down to the school many times to explain that Donny did not know any words and that she and Big Donny could not read well enough to help him.

Jenny and Donny's Home

Jenny and Donny live on the top two, rented, floors of a narrow, three-story wooden house, painted green with white trim. Jenny and Big Donny moved in shortly after they were married in their late teens, and the family has lived there for fourteen years. At one time Big Donny thought about buying the house, but something came up that required their down-payment money, and the opportunity passed. Another tenant, a lone male who travels, lives on the first floor. The house sits sideways on a sloping hill, between a restaurant on the downhill side and a white frame house on the other. Uphill from the neighboring house is a large brick food service company, the corner grocery, and a liquor store. Sidewalks run down both sides of the street where Donny and Timmy are allowed to ride their bikes down the hill into the restaurant's parking lot—*if* Jenny is watching and it is outside of the restaurant's hours. There are no houses on the other side of the street, only a sloping hill down to the large parkway that rims this side of the city. The north-south interstate runs along this parkway. It is across the parkway and under the interstate overpass that Jenny traveled to visit her mother, while she was alive, and other relatives in her old neighborhood, Camp Fairwell. It is also down this interstate highway that Jenny and her family travel to return home most weekends.

At various times, up to three ramshackle vehicles belonging to Big Donny and Jenny are parked in front of the house, a van, a pickup, and a sedan. The entire block is usually lined with parked cars.

The entrance to Jenny and Donny's house is in the back, at the end of a cement walkway that runs along the side of the house. Here there is a small backyard that runs uphill, the boys' primary outdoor play area. A clothesline, usually adorned with drying laundry, runs across half of the yard. A three-sided shed nestles against the side, protecting a collection of plastic toy figures and vehicles belonging to Donny and Timmy. Their bicycles are kept here as well.

Through the back door and up a narrow flight of wooden steps is the entrance to the family's part of the house. This opens into a small kitchen/eating area. The bathroom is off this room along the front of the house and doubles as the laundry room. The living room is the only other room on this floor and is entered through a wide doorway from the kitchen. The top floor of the house holds a large bedroom and a smaller room off of it. Stairs leading to it begin at the outside entrance to the kitchen.

Jenny keeps the house immaculate, with no clutter

or "mess." She apologizes at times when I drop by unannounced for her quilting supplies laid out on the living room floor. The kitchen is the nerve center of the house, where Jenny cooks and the family eats. Over the kitchen table, the phone on the wall has a long cord so Jenny can talk to friends and family while busying herself with chores. A large mahogany chest sits along the back wall of the kitchen and holds important items like photo albums and schoolwork brought home by Donny. Jenny, not really sure what can safely be thrown out, has saved everything brought home since he began school. On the top of the chest is the automatic coffee maker and a microwave. A refrigerator hides behind a curtain in a recess in the wall. During the winter, the burners on the gas stove give off a blue glow and the oven door remains open to contribute to the overall warmth of the room.

The living room contains a heavy wooden suite of furniture with plaid-covered cushions. Most of one wall is taken up by a large fish tank, with its underwater lighting and softly bubbling air tube. Donny and Timmy know the names of the various types of fish in the tank and participate in their care. A large television and videocassette recorder are the focus of attention along another wall. The family owns a respectable library of videotapes. The family Bible rests on top of the television. On the opposite wall, over the sofa, hangs a large confederate flag, surrounded by formal photo portraits of Donny and Timmy in varying stages of infancy and boyhood.

During the winter, the entire family sleeps in the

living room to conserve heat. Pallets and a fold-away bed rest neatly against the remaining wall. Heavy ceramic figurines and lamps provide accessory touches.

The large bedroom upstairs holds a double bed and a bunkbed set. This is where the family sleeps during the summer with the lone window air conditioner. This room is crowded with bureaus, closets, and sewing materials. Over the course of the two years of this study, a makeshift library of children's books, in a bookcase made of orange crates, evolved in a corner of the room. The small back room upstairs is used for storage.

School for Urban Appalachians

School officials in this city have designed a system of "magnet schools" as a response to court-ordered desegregation and as an alternative to busing. This system was designed to keep middle-class children in the city schools and to draw them across neighborhoods, and it has been largely successful. All of the magnet schools are integrated by race. They include foreign language schools, college prep schools, an arts school, and Montessori schools, among others.

Several of the nonmagnet schools in the inner city are mainly all-black or all-white. The school Donny attends, though, is two-thirds black and one-third white. It is a "neighborhood school," one of those remaining schools attended by the many inner-city children whose parents have not chosen a magnet school for them.

Jenny knew nothing about the magnet schools; this school was the one her child was assigned to, so this was where he went. She remembered fondly the school closer to them where Donny attended Head Start. She liked the kids there, and Donny did well: "All A's."

Although Jenny does not say so directly, the presence of so many African Americans at the school makes her nervous. There is a definite level of tension between the two ethnic groups in the inner city, with the African Americans generally experiencing more success in schooling and in achieving social agenda needs through organized political action.[18]

To Jenny, African American children seem pushy and loud and a source of danger to her children. The kids are too rough, she says, and she worries about Donny's safety. She has taught him not to fight but wonders if she made a mistake. He is little for his age, she explains, and the other kids take his papers away from him. I never heard either Jenny or Donny make a racist statement or use an epithet to refer to African Americans, however.

Contrary to popular impression, it is the white urban Appalachian children, not the urban African American, who occupy the bottom of the educational ladder, at least in this city. Dropout rates for urban Appalachians range from 40 percent to near 75 percent in the poorest areas. Absence rates are more than twice that of the system as a whole. Those students who remain in school achieve at a low level relative to national norms and at significantly lower levels than their non-

Appalachian peers, black and white.[19] Data from a local task force study in 1990 showed that children from low-income urban Appalachian neighborhoods have higher rates of identifiable learning problems than children from the city as a whole.[20] This same study indicated that the achievement test scores of urban Appalachian children in grades 1–6 were declining at a rate two to three times greater than that of the district as a whole. In a 1989 survey I conducted with fellow researchers of low-income kindergarten children in the city, the urban Appalachian children scored significantly lower than their African American peers on knowledge specifically related to written language.[21]

When Appalachian children reach adolescence, their dropout rate increases dramatically. Urban Appalachian activists claim that, while poverty is a significant factor, the schools must also assume a large share of the blame.

In an interview for the local newspaper, Michael Maloney, director of the Urban Appalachian Council and longtime activist, explained, "For Appalachian children, there's a deep conflict between the values in school and the values at home. The children aren't prepared to handle this encounter with a large bureaucratic institution. Appalachians expect relationships to be personal; they aren't comfortable with functional relationships."[22]

Jenny, for example, cannot believe that the teacher continues to hand out homework and to criticize Donny for not doing it when the school refuses to put him back into first grade. When I suggest that they think he can do the work, she exclaims, "They should know it! They're not lookin' at the papers. I mean, they're not lookin' at him!"

When urban Appalachian children leave their neighborhood elementary schools for larger junior highs and high schools, they are met with stereotyped caricatures and slurs such as "hillbilly," "white trash," and "river rat." Urban Appalachian informants claim, though, that the biggest cultural clashes come from encounters with the African American culture. In this city, the poor black student population vastly outnumbers the poor white. In school life the urban Appalachian children are marginalized, intimidated, and seek to remain as separate as possible.[23]

Jenny left school a few weeks after beginning seventh grade, her first year at a school outside of her neighborhood.

> See, I couldn't read nothin'. Ever'body else could read, and I was embarrassed to death! But that ain't why [I left school]. Guys would try to fool with me. Black guys and girls, when you pass the classes, always try to jump you, take your lunch money. And I ate good then; I used to weigh 'bout 135 pounds. Nobody took my lunch money! I just fought. That was like an ever'day thing; you got to hold your money and don't let 'em take it.

She added another reason for her decision to leave school at that time:

> Camp Fairwell [her neighborhood] was poor. All the kids in that [elementary] school, we didn't have no

> name brand clothes or nothin' like that, you know. It was all hand-me-down stuff and people [at the junior high] would make fun of you for stuff like that.

Big Donny also left school in the seventh grade, but he had repeated it three times. His story, as related by Jenny, was slightly different. According to Jenny, Big Donny and his two brothers rarely attended school. Both parents worked long hours, leaving the house before the boys were to leave for school and returning after they were expected to get home from school.

"They would just tell them that they went to school, but they didn't."

All of the boys preferred to live down home with their grandmother because of their parents' drinking and fighting. Jenny told one story that took place after a weekend down home during which the boys stayed with their paternal grandmother while their parents stayed with the maternal grandmother.

> It's Sunday, and they're goin' home [to the city] so they got to stop by and pick up [the boys] and they didn't want to go back. Their Grandma'd tell 'em, "Go hide and don't come out until I say." So they'd run down to the woods, down to the caves and stuff, you know, 'til they'd know their mom and dad had to come back 'cause they had to work Monday, you see, or lose their jobs. So they would get to stay down. Grandma said she'd put 'em on a bus [to go to school]. They'd go, and she'd go to town. They'd

> like . . . when the bus goes to different houses picking kids up . . . there was a back door on the back of the bus. They'd just get out of it! And the bus driver wouldn't even know.

Seen through the cultural lens of the mainstream schooling bureaucracy, urban Appalachian children and families are different and deficit-ridden. In a survey of teacher attitudes toward urban Appalachian students and their difficulties, Bobby Ann Starnes found that city teachers held overall negative attitudes toward the children and their families and felt hopeless in their attempts to teach them.[24] The teachers felt that the culture, as a whole, did not value education, that the parents did not know how to parent, and that the parents did not instill a desire for success.

One of Donny's teachers displayed this general negative reaction to urban Appalachian culture to me one day. I had been checking his progress following the end of our formal relationship and was visiting him in school. Countering his teacher's dismal portrayal of his abilities, I stated my belief that he had learned a great deal, given the fact that neither of his parents could read or write. This teacher, who had met Jenny once, passed quick and harsh judgment. "I *knew* she [Jenny] was ignorant as soon as she opened her mouth!" she said.

This reaction must be balanced, though, with those of Ms. Green, Donny's teacher during his second year with me. Ms. Green was a young, soft-spoken, African American woman who cared deeply for her charges. I had heard about Ms. Green from Donny. He mentioned several times how much he liked her, and I could see evidence of her attention on his homework papers. I first met her when Jenny asked me to accompany her to a routine parent/teacher conference. I rode to the school with Jenny and the two boys.

As Ms. Green welcomed us with a smile, the stark contrast between Jenny, in her faded jeans and T-shirt, long hair pulled back in a rubber band, and this tall, pretty woman, dressed in navy slacks and a silk blouse, was highlighted. Donny took Timmy to the back of the room to play with dominoes as Ms. Green offered us both chairs. She stressed that although Donny always tried hard in class, he needed to practice reading more in order to "catch up." Her spontaneous reaction to Jenny's story of how the principal refused to move Donny back to first grade when confronted with his lack of progress revealed her identification with minority life: "That's such a . . . shame! It's a real . . . *injustice!*"

A World Apart within the Inner City

Jenny, Big Donny, Donny, and Timmy are representative of the urban Appalachians who live in poverty in the inner cities. They are members of a cultural minority that has brought its ways of being and of viewing the world from the mountains, where this culture has evolved over many generations. Outside of the mountains, however, their ways have been derided, scorned, and ridiculed. Their mountaineer dialect and accent invite contempt and/or derision from other urban dwellers. They fail to prosper or succeed. They suffer from familial breakdowns, poor health, tragic accidents, and unfulfilled dreams. They are poorly educated and alienated from the school system. They cling to their notion of home in the mountains: there they are real, not caricatures of failure. Along with their kin networks and friends, they live in a world apart within the inner city. Escape down the interstate from an unfriendly, nonaccepting urban community is essential and near at hand. City life makes no more sense to Jenny than she does to its urban mainstream.

3

A World without Print

Current theory posits that young children do not wait to begin to learn to read and write until they start school. Rather, they begin to learn about reading and writing from birth, in their homes and communities, as they observe others using print for various real life purposes and as they begin to "join in" these activities and experiment with their own forms of reading and writing. Thus we often see children of preschool age asking about store signs ("What does that say?"), claiming they can "read" a label or a favorite book, "drawing" their names, and approaching grown-ups with pieces of paper on which they have made marks with the query, "What did I write?"[1] Parents report that they have even overheard older babies and young toddlers in their cribs, babbling in clear "reading" intonation as they turn the pages of little cloth books.

Learning and exploration do not take place in a

vacuum, however. We are able to learn only what we can experience. Language learning, in particular, requires both the existence of language in the environment and the opportunity to interact with language users so that one can work it out—sort out the pragmatic and syntactic rules, learn the vocabulary, and perfect the "sounds" of the language.[2] Emergent literacy researchers and theorists claim that, as children learn oral language through experience and interaction with speech, so do young children learn about print—about written language—as they grow and develop in a literate society such as ours. Much of my own research has been within this paradigm, and I have sought ways to document what it is, linguistically and cognitively, that young children learn about print before school and the ways in which this knowledge affects their success at beginning formal instruction in reading and writing.

When Jenny "plainly told" me that neither she nor Big Donny could read or write, I was anxious to confirm this. If neither Jenny nor Big Donny could read or write *anything* (beyond their names), what place did print have in their home? What were Donny and Timmy learning—or not learning—about written language? This family presented a rare opportunity—in a society such as ours, where print is so pervasive—to explore the role that experiences with print do and do not play in young children's development as literate beings.

Researchers who focus on emergent literacy have stated unequivocally that all children growing up in a literate society learn many important concepts about written language before they begin school. As an emergent literacy researcher, I sought to explore the particulars of this statement. Do all children learn the same concepts, in the same way(s), to the same extent?[3]

Written Language Is Different from Oral

To grasp the significance of the emergent literacy research, one must understand a basic tenet: written language is not simply oral language written down. We do not learn to read and write speech. We learn to read and write written text. Close linguistic study has revealed what most of us intuit. Written language is different from oral language. Related, but different.[4]

These differences can be appreciated if one transcribes true speech; not speech that is *written* to be speech but speech as it occurs. Here is a sample I captured at the breakfast table one morning as my husband and I ate:[5]

Speaker 1	Speaker 2
Today's Monday. . . . Well . . .at	
least if I get this done . . . today,	
. . . as long as I . . . if I don't	
have to match . . . to the sides . . .	
that really shouldn't make any	
difference . . . the way they . . . fiddle	right . . .
with the . . . here . . .	right
. . . . what color . . .	

Speaker 1	Speaker 2
would	
you like the . . . shelves . . . painted?	
	Uh. . . . pr'bly the . . . uh
they're kind of white /??/	. . .
	the 'antique white'. . .
do we have it?	let's use that
where is it	Yeah. . . .
	we do. . . . 'cause you
is there a lot?	brought it up here one
	time.
	remember? I don't
	know
	. . .
	you'll have to check

True speech is so hard to "write" that rendering a faithful transcript is extremely difficult. The tendency is to "hear" the language as it would be written, without the hesitations, fragmentations, repetitions, and so on. Written speech is also extremely hard to "read." One cannot "follow" it; comprehension is difficult. The typical reaction to the task is "You had to be there." And this is true, because speech, or oral language, is used in situations in which both communicative partners are present. They can see each other, read the other's body language, hear the intonation of the speech stream, question and challenge, ask for clarification. Oral language is employed within a shared physical context.

Written language is the opposite. It is used under the

assumption that the two communicants—the writer and the reader—will not share the same physical space when the writing is read. The simple truth of this pragmatic statement is revealed whenever we find ourselves in the uncomfortable position of "listening" to a piece of writing being read, such as at a professional conference or at a meeting. Members of an audience tend to "fade out" whenever a speaker begins to read a paper to them; it is too hard to "follow"; comprehension is difficult. We want the speaker to "speak," to "tell" us what she or he says in the paper. If we had the paper in front of us, we could read it and understand it. We simply find it difficult to comprehend when it is delivered orally. It is as if speaking goes with listening and writing goes with reading. And in fact they do.[6]

Written language differs from oral because we use it to accomplish different tasks—for different purposes. We use it to communicate across time and space. We use it to make permanent a thought, an argument, a story, an emotion. And because language is shaped to suit its purposes, we can look at features of both oral and written language as markers of the type.[7]

Some of these markers seem to be related to pragmatic constraints, some to differences in composing constraints, and others to issues of "style." In general, virtually all of us can "recognize" a language sample as "oral" or "written." This is most obvious when comparing prototypes of each, such as (a) a casual, spontaneous conversation and (b) an academic paper. I predict, however, that most of us could distinguish oral from written even when presented with language samples that tend to share many of the same functions and features, such as (a) a telephone conversation with a good friend and (b) a personal letter to the same friend.

Markers that we use to distinguish between oral and written language include vocabulary, syntax, and reference conventions. Written language tends to employ vocabulary items that have been termed "literary" as opposed to "colloquial," for example, *entrance* rather than *door* and *employ* rather than *use.*

The syntax in written text—including simple children's stories—is more embedded and often transformed. For example, the following construction would rarely be found in speech: *Down the hill ran the green, scaly dragon.* In oral situations, we would more likely encounter something like: *The dragon ran down the hill. He was green and had scales.* Similarly, the dialogue marker—*said the queen*—with the verb position moved to precede the subject is a common occurrence in written text and one that virtually never occurs in speech (with the exception of formal "storytelling"). We would be jarred into concluding that something was "off" if an acquaintance, in relating an event, used a construction such as *"Go to bed," said my mom.*

Finally, within written text, only endophoric references are allowed. Writers may not use a personal pronoun, for example, without providing a referent for it *within* the written text and clearly retrievable by the reader. Speakers can use a pronoun without a referent because they can point to, or by intonation indicate, the man or woman who is being referred to and who is known to the listener. This difference reflects the decontextualized nature of written language as compared with the contextualized nature of oral language.[8]

Emergent Literacy

Given that written language is not simply oral language in print, learning to read and write is not simply a process of learning a written code for speech. Rather, it involves learning to use a different, in many ways "new," language, with all of the complexities of language acquisition that this implies. And children do not wait to learn about this language until they begin formal instruction.

What do children learn about the language of reading and writing during their preinstruction years? Roughly fifteen years of research into this question has yielded some fascinating answers. Young children appear to learn (implicitly, not necessarily explicitly) about written language within roughly three dimensions, each constraining and defining the other (see Figure 1).[9] Everything they learn about written language before schooling is constrained by what they learn about its functions and the values placed on its various forms within their particular sociolinguistic communities and cultures. Within this frame, they learn about the natures, characteristics, and language forms of written language that are used within their cultures. As children participate in literacy events utilizing these forms of written language, they learn that print is a language signifier—that it carries linguistic meaning—and they learn about the ways in which

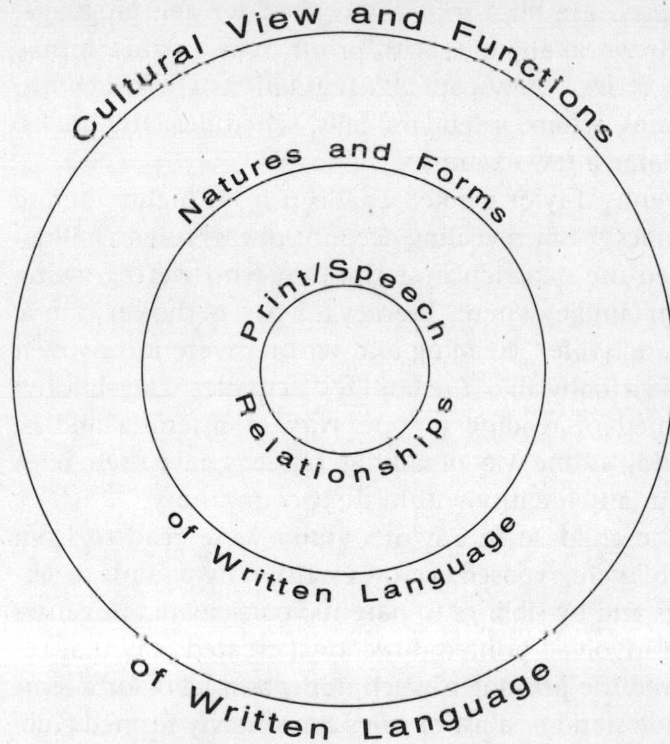

Figure 1 The dimensions of written language knowledge learned by young children through experience, and constrained by cultural practice, prior to formal instruction.

print represents meaning, the "code" and the conventions of encoding and decoding the print.

The Cultural Contexts of Literacy Acquisition

In the United States, where the ability to read and write is essential to economic and social success, many children are born into a world of written language. Their world abounds with print: signs, menus, forms, directories, newspapers, regulations, instructions, memos, letters, calendars, bills, schedules, and books, to name a few examples.

Denny Taylor studied children from highly literate families.[10] Her revealing account of this research illustrated the experience of children who were growing up in families where "literacy is a part of the very fabric of family life." Reading and writing were interwoven into virtually all of the families' activities. The children learned of reading as one way of listening and of writing as one way of talking. Literacy gave them both status and identity within their community.

The children in Taylor's study were read to from birth; were exposed to notes written by parents to siblings and by siblings to parents; participated in games that involved printed directions; created play that required the printing of such items as a label for a lemonade stand or a list of rules for a newly formed club; observed their parents reading books, newspapers, notes from school, and letters from relatives and others; and daily confronted store signs and advertisements both in the environment and on television. It is within this literate context that these children learned much about the nature and forms of written language.

As children experience and utilize written language to serve different functions such as those just described, they sort out the varying forms print can take. Jerome Harste, Virginia Woodward, and Carolyn Burke describe children as young as three years demonstrating that they know that a grocery list is made up of a vertical list of nouns, representing items to be found in a grocery store, while a letter to grandma is composed of sentences that both inquire about grandma's state and report on personal activities.[11] These researchers also cite evidence that young children in Israel will "scribble-write" from right to left using marks that include the various script features typical of written Hebrew.

Elizabeth Sulzby has demonstrated a clear developmental path from oral to written forms of language produced by children rereading favorite storybooks.[12] I have shown that well-read-to five-year-olds implicitly know the syntax, vocabulary, and decontextualized nature of written stories.[13] When asked to "pretend to read" to a doll, they produce stories that are judged to be written in nature as compared with oral narratives they produce. They "sound" as if they are actually reading a book.

As children interact with written language for specified purposes, they begin to sort out and acquire knowledge about the print itself. They learn about (a) the nature of the relationship between speech and print; (b) the conventions of print, for example, linearity, directionality, and word boundaries; and (c) print-related terms like *word* and *letter*.

The research on literacy acquisition has consistently emphasized that it is the interaction with print by the child that enables this learning. Both reading attempts and writing attempts constitute the forms of interaction. As young children attempt to "read" familiar signs, recurring print in favorite books, and their names, they work toward an understanding of print as a code. Similarly, as they engage in writing attempts from "scribble" writing to invented spelling, they become aware of letter features, letter sequences, and the ways in which certain letters map onto speech units.

According to the schema illustrated in Figure 1, therefore, if storybooks are read and valued within a young child's home, this child will learn that written language is used to record stories that are read for pleasure; that written stories have a particular macrostructure that can be used to predict and recall the story; that written narrative uses particular words and sentence structures that people do not use when conversing; and that print stands for language and can be recorded and decoded via a particular system that in English is alphabetic.[14] This child will learn about the function, nature, and conventions of written stories. Another child who comes from a home where only the Koran is read aloud, and no other uses of print are available, will learn about the function, nature, and conventions of the written Koran but not about written stories. Children learn about what they experience and participate in within their particular sociolinguistic cultures.

Written language, then, is phenomenon; it is not ubiquitous to all; it is apparent in the environment only to the extent that it is recognized or noticed. It is recognized, or noticed, only to the extent that it is used by fellow members of one's sociocultural/sociolinguistic group.

Donny and Timmy's World: Phenomenologically Almost Print-Free

Donny and Timmy's world was virtually void of functional literacy events beyond the signing of names and an occasional minimal mark on a wall calendar. By this I mean that no one in their immediate family—no one in their home—used print for any other purpose. Neither Jenny nor Big Donny read or wrote *anything* beyond familiar names and simple marks for notations on the calendar.

For a long time I refused to believe Jenny's statement that neither she nor Big Donny could "read a lick." During our first session in the Literacy Center, I asked her to look through a newspaper and its advertisements to find something she could read. With great difficulty, she could decode a few words in a story accompanied by a picture. She identified a few advertised items that were "things that I know what they mean even if I can't read the words."

I sent her home with the assignment to write down words she could read off of household products in her home. She returned with a list of items (see Figure 2). She could read these to me with difficulty and assured me that she could do this only because she remembered writing them down on the list. "Now if they're on somethin' different, say like *Crisco,* if the word was on somethin' else, I wouldn't know it." She commented that she didn't know how to spell *coffee* since all that was on the can were the words *Maxwell House.*

Over the span of our time together, I confirmed Jen-

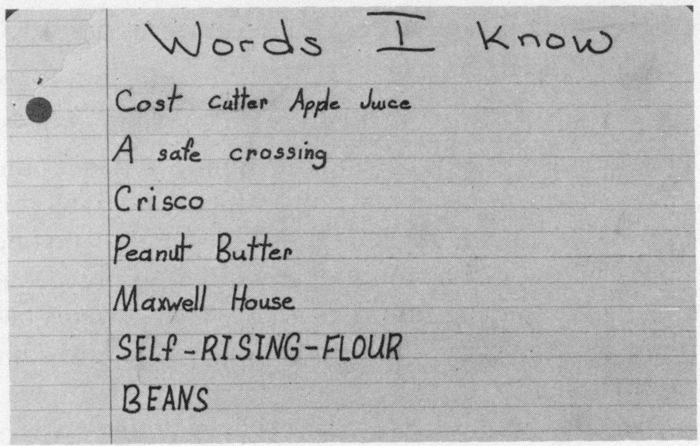

Figure 2 Words Jenny could read from items in her kitchen.

ny's claim of nonliteracy. Outside of the home, Jenny used physical markers to locate stores, offices, and items on grocery shelves. She noted size of buildings, colors and shapes of signs, and logos.

These strategies were illustrated for me one day when she related her problems finding the vet's office because it had moved to a new location. Although she had followed the directions given to her over the phone (with important physical landmarks elicited by her), she could not find the office. She returned home and called. With this call, she discovered that they had changed their sign and requested a specific description of the shape of the sign (square), what colors were on it (white and bordered with black), and size (larger than the last one). At no time did she request information about the content, or words, on the sign; that would have been irrelevant information for her.

Jenny tended to shop always in the same few stores, where she was familiar with the arrangement of products. The few times she entered new stores, she usually took a friend with her to help her find what she needed. I accompanied her on several occasions as she sought to purchase items she had seen in the Literacy Center. Looking for alphabet cards, we visited a teacher supply store. Jenny needed my help to decode all print placed to direct shoppers, print on product packages, and print indicating prices. She disliked having to depend on others in this way, and this aversion to dependency was one of her motivations for learning to read.

Within their home, both Big Donny and Jenny functioned without print. Jenny cooked and cleaned from knowledge acquired orally and through experience. The same was true for her quilting activities. She never consulted cookbooks or written recipes from other sources. She never read directions for preparation from food packaging. Whenever she needed this type of information, she would consult friends or family, often over the telephone. When given directions or information, she never wrote it down, relying instead on her memory. If she forgot a particular direction, she would contact her informant again or call someone else.

Big Donny worked as a roofer, when he could find work, and he too used skills and knowledge acquired through experience. He always worked with a contractor or "boss" who told him what to do, when, and where. He did not need to read or write on the jobs he took on. At home Big Donny watched television, including the many videotapes he purchased. Many of these tapes were on natural history or historical topics—two areas of interest to Big Donny. His other source of leisure within the home was drawing. He was a "good drawer," according to Donny, and often drew pictures as gifts for the two boys. His drawing paper and pencils were stored on top of the refrigerator and considered off limits to the rest of the family.

On the family's many trips down home, print was similarly unnecessary. The route on the interstate was familiar from childhood, including the exit and subsequent journey down rural roads. When Jenny was pressed by me, late in the study, for her personal reasons for learning to read, she did say that it would be nice to be able to read the road signs during these trips, just to know what towns they were passing along the way. This was not a pressing concern for her, however.

Nor did the family's activities while down home focus on reading or writing. Rather, the family members engaged in "four-wheelin'," hunting, fishing, visiting with friends and family, cooking, gardening, sewing, and canning.

Big Donny's older brother and his wife lived permanently down home, and the visits centered around their house and one nearby built for Big Donny and Jenny to use. James and Karen were both literate and their children were successful in school. Their older daughter was training to be a nurse during this time. Karen made some books and magazines available and often took on the responsibility of monitoring Donny's homework during extended visits. No one from Jenny and Big Donny's family, though, paid any attention to these sources of print. According to Jenny, whether one could read or write was irrelevant among extended family members or groups of friends.

Literacy Objects Do Not Equal Use

One of the strategies literacy researchers use to measure functional literacy in homes is to make note of artifacts tied to reading and writing. In Jenny's and Donny's home, this strategy did not work. Although there was no evidence of magazines, newspapers, or libraries of well-worn books in the home, it did contain printed material. As noted earlier, the family Bible was prominently displayed on top of the television. There were also two prints on the living room walls with religious sayings appearing in a cross stitch design. In the kitchen, a calendar hung underneath the telephone. During my first visit, Jenny brought down from an upstairs closet two large cardboard boxes filled with children's books. On subsequent visits, she showed me some old books Big Donny had salvaged from building projects. These were also stored upstairs. Thus one could say that this was a home with books.

No one, however, could, or did, read any of these books. The Bible had been in Jenny's family for generations, and it was considered an inherent part of any home. Issues of morality or ethics were often settled by reference to the Bible, but no one in the home could actually read any part of it. Jenny's knowledge of its content had been acquired orally and she transmitted it orally to her children and other adults.

Jenny told me that she had gotten the children's

books from relatives or from Goodwill. She had heard that it was important for children to be read to and to have books in the home. She had tried to read out of them to Donny and Timmy but was unable to do so. She had "pieced out" one simple book, but the kids were tired of it and wanted other ones. Big Donny would occasionally "read" these books to the boys by "putting in his own words" to go with the pictures. Jenny objected to this on ethical grounds but would occasionally do it too, when pressed by the kids. When she did this, though, she always told them that she wasn't "really reading" the book. Both boys had their favorites among these books, chosen according to the pictures they liked best. Jenny reported that the books were always stored in the closet and were brought out on occasion to sort through before being packed up again and put away.

The unavailability of print for the family was highlighted for me the day Jenny brought out the collection of old—some of them may have been valuable antiques—books salvaged from building projects by Big Donny. These were large, leatherbound volumes with the edge of their pages gilded in gold. Jenny brought them out to ask me what type of books they were. I looked through two of them, but could not help her because they were written in German. When I told Jenny that I could not read them either, she was surprised. She had assumed that they were simply like all of the other texts she could not read: filled with confusing letters and words. We speculated together on whether or not one was a Bible, based on some of the illustrations. She wondered whether the other one might be an encyclopedia since the text seemed to be arranged like one, although she was not really sure what an encyclopedia was and asked me to explain it to her.

Jenny did make minimal use of print to keep track of appointments and to pay household bills. The calendar under the telephone on the kitchen wall often showed individual numbers or letters printed on the daily squares. Jenny explained that occasionally she would make a mark on the calendar to help her remember to apply for food stamps or to appear for a teacher conference. They were minimal marks, however, and the bulk of the to-be-remembered item was stored in Jenny's head. In spite of these occasional notations, Jenny several times missed appointments when she would forget to check the calendar.

The kitchen table rested against the wall directly under the calendar, and I always saw a small pile of household bills on it. I finally asked her how she read the bills: how did she know whom to pay, how much, and when? She acknowledged that Carol, her sister-in-law who lived up the hill, or Wanda, her sister, would usually come over to help her. She was able, she said, to read the part that said how much she owed but could not read the other parts explaining the charges. She always paid with cash, and usually in person. A few times, when Karen and James were up visiting from down home, they would help her fill out the forms and mail them for her.

The Effect on Donny and Timmy

Phenomenologically, Donny and Timmy were not growing up in a literate environment. Although they lived in a home situated in a city situated in a country that contained many forms and functions for print, they did not experience it. They did not notice it around them; they did not understand its uses. Their world functioned without written language.

In terms of the emergent literacy conceptual framework (see Figure 1), Donny and his younger brother Timmy learned very little about written language during their preschool years. The uses to which their parents put print framed what Donny had been able to learn by the time I met him—names, minimal marks, and pretend-reading of books with oral language. Beyond this, however, the boys virtually failed to identify print as functional. Several incidents in the Literacy Center illustrated this vividly for me.

One day in the Center, I informed Donny that I was about to leave on a two-week trip to England and, therefore, could not meet with him until I returned. To make up for missing our sessions, I promised to send him a postcard from London.

"What's that?" he wanted to know. I told him that a postcard was like a letter but with a picture on it, usually from the place from which you are sending it. He indicated no understanding of what a letter was.

"I'll buy a postcard with a picture of London Bridge on it," I continued (he knew the nursery rhyme "London Bridge Is Falling Down"), "and on the back of the card I'll write a message to you. It will be like me talking to you from far away."

His polite nod was accompanied with a dismissive shrug. I later mentioned to Jenny that Donny did not know about postcards or letters.

"It's true," she said. "No one writes to us 'cause they all know we can't read it." Although the family did receive mail, no one in the home ever read it. Therefore this was a functional use of written language unknown to Donny.

I did send several postcards from London to both Donny and Jenny after forewarning them to look for them. The messages I wrote could be read by both of them at that time in their instruction, I felt. When I returned I inquired about their receipt. Donny had forgotten about them, and Jenny denied that they had ever been delivered. When I described the pictures on them (one of Donny's had been of a red-coated guard with a tall black fur hat), Jenny did vaguely remember seeing such a picture.

"But I never would'a thought to turn it over to see some writin' to me!" she confessed.

On another occasion in the Literacy Center, a suggestion from me led to a further revelation of the extent to which Donny failed to conceptually understand the functional basis of written language. Donny's favorite activities involved making things with his hands. He always rushed into the Center ahead of his mother to the writing area, where he would quickly put together something with the paper, scissors, glue, and string. On one winter day in the first year of our relationship, he proceeded to fold, cut, glue, staple, and produce a kite by the time I had finished greeting Jenny and getting her settled. Other children were evidencing much interest in making a similar kite, and I suggested to Donny that he write a book—with my help—to explain how to make a kite.

"We could add it to the library here in the Center," I explained, "and then whenever someone wants to make a kite like this, they can read the book and do it."

Donny looked at me as if I were speaking in a different language. "Why," he gently explained to me, "I'll just *show* them how to make it."

Taking this opportunity to demonstrate the value of written language over oral, I replied, "Well, you may not be here when someone—who comes to the Center at a different time—wants to make the kite."

"Then, I'll show you, and you can show them," he concluded. Skills, such as making a kite, were acquired through personal experience, demonstration, and oral explanation in Donny's world. Print played no part.

After Schooling

Donny had completed two years of schooling by the time we met. What was the effect of instruction and school activities on his conceptual knowledge base regarding written language? There was some evidence that he had acquired some simple, if incomplete, information regarding the functional nature of print from school. He knew that print could encode names (initially experienced and later reinforced in his home)—in particular, his first name. He could write his name when asked and could read it when someone else pointed it out to him. He could write nothing else, however.

Donny also knew that within the context of a book, print was 'read.' He revealed this early in our association when as we looked through a children's book, he pointed to a page with pictures but no words and commented, "This is a thinkin' page!" and pointed to the following page that contained words and said, "This is a readin' page!" Again, this was a concept that had been introduced in his home.

The powerful interplay between home and school learning was evidenced in Donny's belief of what constituted "readin'." When asked to read a page of print, he readily looked at the pictures and provided his "own words," just as his parents did at home. These words could change from one reading to the next because in his conceptual network, print did not play the role of holding language static. A "reader" rendered oral language—which could be quite rich—in the context of pictures within a book. The black marks that we call 'print' were irrelevant; they could have been fly specks for all they had to do with the language one used when reading.

Donny had also learned a school-type use of written language that, in the world of people's lives, is considered more of a prerequisite to use: he knew that letters were named and printed as isolated units of the "alphabet." He had not completely mastered this by the beginning of second grade, but he could accurately recognize about two-thirds of the letters in the alphabet and accurately reproduce about 90 percent of those. Although he would never choose to do this on his own, he could perform these tasks when directed to by a teacher.

When we first met, Donny could "do school" on a surface level. He had learned to fill in blanks of worksheets, circle words on worksheets, pay attention to the teacher, and "follow along" in his book as the teacher, or someone else, read. Early in the study, I observed him one day in his second-grade classroom. His teacher was reading a story to the class while the children followed in their own copies of the book. At least, this was the teacher's intention. The majority of the children, however, were scuffling, calling out, crawling around the room, and laughing and talking together. Donny, though, sat quietly in his seat. His eyes were focused on the pages of his book, and he remembered to move them at times and occasionally turn the pages—which never quite matched those his teacher was reading from.

Finally, the young, frustrated teacher gave up reading and began a lesson on "telephone manners," which called for some role playing. This increased the attention of most of the children. During this time, though, Donny had his head buried under the lift-up top of his desk and was engaged in cleaning and ordering its contents.

The "telephone manners" lesson soon led to a worksheet event, and the teacher handed each child a mimeographed page with a list of words at the top and a series of numbered sentences below. Each sentence had a blank in it that the children were to fill in with one of the listed words. The teacher instructed them to "write the words that fit in the blanks." She led the class through the words and each sentence orally, giving them the answers. Unfortunately, Donny's head was still buried in his desk.

When the children began to fill in the blanks with pencils, though, he quickly began work. As I watched in amused consternation, he measured each word with his two index fingers, moved them to the blanks and matched word to sentence according to the perceived "fit." He then copied the word into the blank. Retrieving the paper later, I confirmed that none of the sentences made sense as he had completed them. But that was irrelevant to Donny; he had completed the task as he had interpreted its demands: matching objects by length—"fitting" words to blanks.

The emergent literacy framework indicates that children will learn about the natures and forms of written language according to those functions they see print fulfilling in their lives. Donny had thus learned about letters and form as these applied to the writing of his name and to the recognition and printing of the letters of the alphabet. He had, however, almost no implicit notions of the vocabulary, syntax, or decontextualized nature of written language as found in books, letters, environmental signs, written directions, or personal notices.

The most startling insight for me as I worked with

Donny and analyzed the data I collected over the two years was that for Donny, print did not signify; it did not code his world; it was not linguistically meaningful. Donny did not *notice* the print around him; it did not emerge perceptually from the background of his life. He never traveled the route of other children from literate homes who, for example, progress from first noticing the "Stop" sign and its role in directing drivers to stop, to understanding that the letters s-t-o-p "say" *Stop*. In answer to my questioning, Jenny reported that neither child ever asked about what the words or print in their environment "said." Rather, the children learned to use the symbols their parents used: physical landmarks, colors, and shapes.

If we consider Donny and Timmy in terms of the inner dimension of the emergent literacy conceptual framework, we find that the boys had no sense that print operates as a code. Without the context of functional uses of print in their world, they never thought to explore its symbolic nature through pretend readings or writing attempts during their preschool years. Paper and pencils in the home were not tools for writing to Donny and Timmy. If they were available, they were for drawing like their dad did. The irrelevancy of instruction in school on the code nature of print will be addressed in Chapter 4. Its ineffectual nature was obvious.

At the beginning of his second-grade year, Donny did not know all of the names of the letters of the alphabet. He did not know what a printed "word" was in the sense of matching an oral word with a printed word bounded by white space; when he "read" a memorized text of *Three kangaroos live here,* for example, he ran his fingers under *live here* as he "read" the last two syllables of *kangaroo.* He did not know what a "letter" was as distinguished from other printed marks such as periods and commas; he did not know that his oral words could be written down; rather he believed that only "book words" could be copied (this belief was also held by his mother regarding her own language, as we shall see).

At the beginning of his second-grade year, Donny could read only his first name and, with prodding and time to reflect, the word *the.* He could write only his first name. Like any other seven-year-old with at least normal intelligence, he had conceptualized his world as he had experienced it. When he began first grade, at age six, he had made sense of his instruction as it fit with his already-held beliefs, understandings, and skills. The marginal impact of instruction in reading and writing reflected the wide gap between his world without print and that assumed by the schools.

4

Becoming Literate: Donny

Donny and Jenny had both failed to learn to read and write from what can be termed "traditional, skills-based" instruction. Jenny's early years in school were not available to me for study. I could only record her few memories of them. Her overriding memory was one of frustration and alienation:

> Most of my friends around me could read. I just copied from their papers. 'Cause I couldn't. You know like when you're first meetin', you would ask. 'Cause like the teacher, they would explain what to do and then figure they would explain it once, they wouldn't have to go over it again. You should know what they're talking about. And I'd raise my hand, and a lot of times, they'd say, "Put your hand down." You know, they don't want to listen to you. So you get stuck and then you're embarrassed to ask . . . to raise your hand again 'cause all the kids are laughin' at you. So you won't do it again. That's the way I did anyway.

When we met, however, Donny and Jenny were both attending school, and I could observe them in these settings and share their assignments and evaluations. Jenny was beginning her third year of fairly regular attendance at a community-based adult school, staffed by volunteers. Her express goal in attending this program was to learn to read. She shared with me the work she did at these sessions early in the study, arriving at the Literacy Center one day with about six workbooks. Sitting alongside me, she explained that she usually "worked through" a page or two during each session. She had completed the workbooks she brought to show me.

Still trying to grasp the extent of her reading ability, I eagerly asked her to read from one of the books. The workbooks were organized so that each page contained from two to three paragraphs of text, followed by questions. The topics centered on adult issues such as shopping or working. Jenny chose a page that contained a passage written on about a fourth-grade level. She read haltingly, word by word. She miscued on several "small" words, reading *which* for *with*, for example, and was unable to self-correct. When I gave her these words she continued on in her word-by-word manner without rereading the sentence or phrase.

As she read, I got the clear impression that she viewed the task of reading as one of remembering isolated words, one at a time, with no sense of language structure or meaning. This was reinforced when she commented after finishing the passage,

> I can read in here [the workbook] only because I been in 'em for so long. And like some of the words I don't know, I just stop a minute and think, or try to think—figure it—figure it out, and then I could go on.

When I asked her how she would try to figure it out, she said,

> Well, I can read 'em now. O.K., like *father*, I couldn't read that for the longest time. And I had a paper. The words that was hard for me that I didn't know? I had 'em written down. And then when I would go to it, somehow I would remember it by looking at this paper, in the way I had 'em written down. And then I'd just go on.

She reiterated her earlier statement regarding the words she had copied off of items in her kitchen: "I can read 'em in here [the workbook], but if they're anywheres else, I don't know 'em."

Traditional skills-based reading instruction assumes that one learns to read by learning component skills of reading separately and practicing these skills to mastery.[1] These skills are presented and learned in a structured sequence from simple to higher order. In skills-based reading instruction, the learner reads from materials especially written to teach the component skills of reading, which can be broadly summarized as decoding (through phonic and word analysis knowledge) and comprehension (including vocabulary study). The skills are viewed as discrete enough to teach and learn separately, and the reading material is used for practice both in isolated skills and in using learned skills in combination. The assumption is that one first learns to read (a period assigned to the kindergarten through third grade) and then reads to learn (from fourth grade on up).[2] Learning to write is viewed as a separate process, made up of its own component discrete skills.

It did not take a skilled diagnostician to conclude that a fresh look at the type of instruction needed by Jenny and Donny was called for. Neither had made any real progress toward full literacy under their skills-based curriculums after one year for Donny and a total of ten years for Jenny.[3] As the teacher, I felt it my responsibility to discover and provide instruction from which each learner could benefit. Hence I looked for ways to help Donny and Jenny learn to read and write.

In Donny's case, research findings in emergent literacy suggested clear avenues for instruction. Given the virtual nonliteracy of his home and the absence of literacy knowledge I observed in him during his first few times at the Center, he seemed likely to fail to make any sense of traditional reading/writing instruction until he had built the requisite conceptual understandings of written language. This meant that he must become involved with many varied literacy events within a setting rich with functional uses of print. He must observe, participate in, and experiment with written language being used for many different real-life purposes. He would be able to learn the component skills of reading and writing only after he had built for himself a conceptual base that included the knowledge that print is linguistically meaningful and that it is an integral part of people's lives, allowing many different types of communication, and that it is codelike in the sense that one can learn its symbols by applying knowledge of the language it encodes to "read" and "write" it.[4]

Jenny was beyond this sort of work because she already controlled many of these concepts; she simply did not use them. At present, therefore, she could not learn by "sitting alongside" while I taught Donny. For close to a year and a half, Jenny's and Donny's developmental paths differed before eventually converging to the point where they could work together.

Donny

The Literacy Center provided the literate environment for Donny's conceptual work. It was a large room stocked with many books of all types and levels. There were also magazines and newspapers available. The walls were covered with printed notices, riddles, posters "advertising" favorite books, and directions to ongoing games related to books. Many of these had been created by the children. Also centrally displayed and available for reading were self-published books written by the learners in the Center. The children were encouraged to read and write for their own, self-directed purposes. Writing was encouraged through the availability of paper, blank journals, stationery with envelopes, note pads, message forms, blackboard, computers, pens, pencils, markers, crayons, and an array of stick-on letters and shapes, glue, and string.

A wide selection of books, stories, and songs on audiotape was available for listening with tape players and earphones.

The room is irregularly shaped, providing nooks and crannies for reading and writing alone or with small groups. The children who attend the Center work one-to-one with a tutor/teacher for one hour twice a week after school.

The instruction and supporting theory embodied in the Literacy Center differed in several important ways from the skills-based instruction that Donny and Jenny had previously experienced. Grounded in psycholinguistic theory of language acquisition, the instruction presupposed several learning principles:[5] (a) Language is learned as it is used to fulfill meaningful, authentic functions and cannot be learned for its own sake, in isolation from function; (b) the components (sounds, syntax, semantics, pragmatics) of language are learned as they transact synergistically during authentic use, not separately to mastery; and (c) language development proceeds recursively in an "ever-widening variety of contexts,"[6] not from simple to higher order sequentially.

Whereas in skills-based instruction children read from materials specially written to teach sequenced skills, in the Literacy Center children read from materials written to fulfill authentic functions of print, such as children's literature, informational notices and tracts, written directions for games or scientific experiments, and so on. The reading and writing is driven by the function served and not, predominantly, to learn to read and write. This is in contrast to the skills-based belief that one first learns to read and then reads to learn (form preceding function).

Further, reading instruction and writing instruction are seen as complementary because they are complementary language processes, that is, one writes for a reader and reads from a writer. Many of the strategies learned for writing help the writer read and comprehend written text and vice versa. A fuller description of the theory behind the activities in the Literacy Center and the roles of the teachers can be found in the Appendix.

During his sessions in the Center, Donny was always surrounded by children and adults reading and writing for many and varied functional reasons. As a social being, he could not help but be drawn in by this and begin to participate. I was his teacher, and this one-to-one relationship, as well as the draw of the literate activities going on around him, prevented Donny from burying his head in a desk as he had done in his classroom.

Feeling that Donny had years of being read to to make up, I devoted time each session to this activity. Also feeling the press of time to help him gain ground as a reader and writer, I read to him from two types of books—children's storybooks, the texts of which were beyond the level for beginning reading, and books written in predictable, less complex, language for his initial foray into actual reading on his own. He loved to be read to and always followed the story line with interest and intelligence, interacting freely with me with comments on the characters and predictions about the unfolding plot.

To demonstrate that printed symbols coded the language being read, I began a systematic program of activity with the simple predictable books. I would read the book through to him several times. I would then have him read aloud with me. He had basically memorized the text by this time and was not really reading the words. I would then take a photocopied version of the text pages and, page by page, have him read the text, cut out the sentences, order them, and read them again to check on the ordering. Although he enjoyed the cutting and ordering, this project was hard work for Donny, focusing him on the actual print for the first time. He tired easily at this so I kept these sessions short. As time went on, I had him cut apart the words in the sentences and rebuild the text at the sentence level. During all of this I was explicitly explaining concepts of "sentence," "word," and "letter," and Donny was exploring and manipulating these concepts with his eyes, voice, scissors, and hands.

From a different perspective, he explored the same concepts during writing activities. At first Donny would only copy words from books during writing time, indicating a belief that there was no other way to write. He did this with several of the short predictable books before he agreed to move to encoding his own words.

The availability of the paper and various writing instruments plus the observed activity around him soon proved interesting to Donny. He began to experiment with the different markers and pens, drawing geometric shapes and isolated letters as well as writing his name in various colors, sizes, and shapes. As he saw other children creating their own stories and books, he decided to try it. It was through these writing events that the "big picture" concept of the intentionality of print was concretely demonstrated for him and initially grasped by him.

To understand that print signifies linguistically, one must comprehend the real link between personal meanings and print; it must code *your* world and you must grasp that fact. Donny's lack of connection between his own world and print remained a deep concern of mine.

Initially, either frightened of being wrong or having absolutely no idea of how to begin, Donny absolutely refused to experiment with writing beyond the letter level. I therefore scribed for him as he dictated stories or real-life accounts of adventures. He had a lively imagination, and one could never be sure whether he was encoding fact or fiction or a blend of the two. One of his first dictations was the following, which he told me was about a recent trip down home:

> I did not catch a deer. I went over there to feed them. My Dad tipped the four-wheeler. Me and my friends went to the creek. My friend rode me on his four-wheeler. Big Earl rode me on his four-wheeler. Little Earl shot a deer. Cecil shot two deers. Little Earl went hunting. That's the first time he went hunting.

As with the small, predictable books, Donny, under my guidance, read over his stories, pointing at the words and working on the concepts of "word," "letter," "sentence," and punctuation marks.

One day Donny was ready to build an initial, tenuous bridge between himself and print. I had sent him to the writing table "to write something to share" while I worked with Jenny for a few minutes. Usually he would either experiment with the markers or create objects out of paper during these times, waiting for me to write for him. This time, though, he took seriously our directive, "Spell it the way you hear it." He came rushing over to his mother and me with his journal outstretched in his hand and a pleased glow on his face. "I wrote something! Didn't I?" he exclaimed and queried at the same time. I looked at his writing, and he had indeed written something:

IMI

"I am I!" he read. "I am I!"

"Yes, you are!" I responded with delight. "And you can write!"

Donny had represented himself in print. He had placed himself within a literate world, albeit tentatively and with great caution. My fervent hope was that this move be not temporary but rather the beginning of a real move into literacy.

The next several months were spent trying to solidify this conceptual beginning. Each session, Donny dictated stories and read his own stories, experimented with his own writing and spelling, listened to rich children's literature, and read progressively more complex text from the beginning reading books. Throughout all of these activities, I was explicitly focusing him on important concepts basic to learning to read and write: an utterance is represented in writing with specific individual words that are separated by white space; these words are made up of individual letters that must be placed in a specific order per word; individually, these letters have "names," and within words, they represent "sounds" that are present in our speech when we say the words aloud.

And, as described earlier, I was constantly attempting to expand Donny's knowledge and understanding of the many ways in which written language functions in the world. I explained and sent postcards to him; I described and helped him produce storybooks and "how to" books; I located and shared written information from reference books to answer his many questions about the world; I brought in newspapers and together we found and read stories about the space shuttle, the Gulf War, and advertisements for four-wheelers; as we walked through the hallways and along the streets, I pointed out environmental print like the word *Phone* on the pay phone and the word *Men* on the bathroom down the hall. As with the stories and writing activities, I used these events to point out to Donny the relationships between print and speech, letters and words.

An early sign of progress was reported by Jenny just before Christmas break: Donny was now getting three to four words right on his weekly spelling tests at school. Given the basic conceptual understanding that print codes speech using groups of individual letters to represent it within words, he was able to "hang on to" invariant spellings for the first time in his life.

During these early months of our work together, Donny displayed several behaviors that were to persist throughout the two years. First of all, Donny responded to the "choice" element of the Center by enthusiastically demonstrating his predilection for "making things." At every opportunity, he would cut and paste, shape and glue, fold and staple; paper for Donny was for "makin' things." This meant that, while we did indeed engage in the many reading and writing activities just described, the impetus was always mine, and a great deal of my time was spent focusing and refocusing Donny on the print aspect of the activities.

Second, Donny proved to be incredibly adept at ignoring the print I was attempting to point out. Always polite, he nevertheless engaged in clear passive-aggressive resistance to literacy-focused activities. Over time, this took the form of conscious helplessness. He truly enjoyed listening to stories and talking about them. He equally enjoyed dictating stories for me to write. What he did not want to do was to read anything himself or to write on his own. When prompted to read a message from another child or text in a book, he would urge, "*You* do it." His relatively rare occasions of self-directed reading and writing were truly cause for celebration by me.

Phonemic Understanding

Many young children achieve conceptual understanding of the phonemic nature of written English through the activity of "invented spelling." By attempting to encode their language in print, learners move developmentally toward a full understanding of the relationship between letters and sounds and meaning. Although much of this conceptual work takes place before the years of schooling for children from rich literacy environments, studies have shown that encouraging this activity in classrooms is especially beneficial to those children who fall into the lower quartiles of achievement in the early school years.[7] I was therefore eager for Donny to begin to engage in his own invented spellings. He was extremely reluctant to do so, however, with the exception of the "IMI" episode.

When Donny began to make encoding attempts, they were not with any of the many pencils, pens, or markers. He chose, instead, to use the stick-on letters available in the writing center. Again while I was talking to Jenny (and hence unavailable for help), he chose to "make" a word. Carefully selecting letters from the sheet of stick-ons, he created:

AXRA

When asked what it said, he proclaimed, "X-ray." Within his Appalachian dialect, this encoding was phonemically accurate and complete, that is, there were no missing "sounds."

He continued to create individual words in this manner during successive sessions. Within a month, he moved to the sentence level with the following, all letters chosen from the stick-on sheets:

You R mi fran

"Thank you," I said, as I read his "writing." "You are my friend, too."

Although the instances of self-directed writing using his own spellings remained rare, I could tell from the few he did that he understood the phonemic base of printed English. This, combined with his increased exposure to the ways in which written language functions in life, led me to conclude that he was now ready for systematic instruction in the ways in which "sounds" map onto print—phonics.

While there is considerable debate over the efficacy of teaching phonics to beginning readers and writers, I believe that explicit instruction in this aspect of the reading/writing process is quite beneficial for most learners, especially those who experience problems.[8] This instruction must be only a piece of a larger literacy curriculum, though, one that stresses, through numerous demonstrations and activities, that the purposes for reading and writing are many and that the goal of decoding and encoding thought and language through print is to gain access to the underlying meaning. It is only within this conceptual, intentional frame that learning the basics of the sound/symbol match makes sense to learners and thus becomes knowledge to be grasped and used. Phonics instruction needs to be responsive to individual needs. It should be employed only to the point at which the learner is reading independently and well enough so that new skills and strategies are learned mainly through the process of reading itself.

Donny, of course, had been "exposed" to a great deal of phonics instruction over his, by now, almost two years of schooling. My hypothesis about its striking failure to help him learn to read or write was that it was essentially meaningless—nonsensical—to him. If, as I surmised, print did not signify for Donny, then it was not a "code" for him. Asking him to learn to "read" those funny marks on a page by applying "decoding" rules was equivalent to expecting people to learn to "read" the patterns of branches in trees. Donny did not even notice, for the most part, the print around him. When it was pointed out to him, he was not sure what to take note of; he did not see patterns because he did not *see* it enough in a regularized way.

Donny did, however, remember a few, isolated "facts" from his phonics lessons at school. He knew the sounds associated with most of the consonants. The ones he did not know revealed an early conceptual understanding, one that assigns a "sound" to a letter based on the letter name. He tended, for example, to write a 'Y' when encoding a /w/ sound (notice that the lips form in the same way when saying the letter name 'Y' as they do when making the sound of /w/ as in *witch*).

When his attention was directed to print, Donny had no way of decoding a word beyond the initial letter, usually a consonant. Accordingly, I began focused phonics lessons with the vowel sounds. The lessons followed the typical sequence, first presenting the "short" vowel sounds with surrounding consonants first (as in *Dad, pet, dog*) and progressing to "long" vowel sounds *(date, seat, load)* along with consonant blends *(drag, thing)*. Donny liked to do this work at the blackboard where he could write with chalk in large strokes.

The phonics work usually took up about one quarter of each session, the rest devoted to listening to text read by me or on a tape, writing events, and reading familiar text. Donny caught on to the principles quickly and proved adept at both writing words I dictated to him and reading those I wrote for him. This work began in the spring of the first year and continued until the end of the second year.

An impressive number of studies have concluded that learners must understand the phonemic nature of printed English if they are to become independent readers.[9] It is the lack of this knowledge, often termed *phonemic awareness*, that accounts for most instances of reading failure, according to many researchers and educators. One indication that learners firmly control this conceptual knowledge is their ability to manipulate the phonemes within words, thus indicating the psychological reality to the learner of the phoneme. If, for example, a learner can regularly "move" the beginning phoneme of a word to the end and pronounce it, as in the old linguistic game of "Pig Latin" (ig-pay ent-way ome-hay), then a grasp of phonemic awareness can be assumed.

As I increasingly focused Donny on the graphophonemic aspect of print, I looked for evidence that he did or did not possess phonemic awareness. We played games at the blackboard during which I would dictate phonetically regular words for him to encode. I would then ask him to move or replace beginning, middle, and end sounds in the words to make new words, for example, "Change the word *run* to *bun*." "Make *like* say *lake.*" "Make *lake* say *cake.*" "Move the beginning sound of *pit* to the end and the end sound of *pit* to the beginning. What word do you have?" He could perform these manipulations, evidencing no confusion on the concept of a phoneme. He also relished challenging me with turnabout requests. I concluded that this knowledge was in place; whether or not he would use it to learn to read was still unknown.

Gap between Development and Curriculum

As Donny neared the end of his first year in the Center and his second-grade year in school, I could see a great deal of growth. His school, however, saw a total failure. To explain the school's poor perception of Donny's growth as a reader/writer, it is necessary to view him through the lens used by the school—the reading/writing curriculum. The basal reading and language arts curriculum used in all classrooms in the district was a highly regarded and typical one. When Donny began formal schooling at the start of grade 1, he was provided instruction which assumed that he and his classmates possessed a number of conceptual understandings about print. The children were assumed to understand that print signifies linguistically and that it is used to fulfill many different functions in the world. The children were also assumed to know that in English, the print code is alphabetic, with individual letters representing isolable phonemes. It was also assumed that the children knew of the many conventions of print. These included the left-to-right eye sweep with return to left margin of the following line; the top-to-bottom ordering of lines of print; the eye-to-voice match with individual words; and the concepts of "word," "letter," and "sound." We can conclude that this knowledge was assumed by the curriculum because the curriculum included no assessment of or instruction in these concepts. Further, the skills included for teaching in the curriculum for first grade were based on these understandings.

During Donny's year in first grade, the teacher taught the curriculum for reading and writing. The word-reading skills, which were taught in order, included: consonant sounds—beginning, final and medial; vowel sounds—short, long, diphthongs, r-controlled, and variant forms; word identification using context and phonics; letter names, rhyming words; phonograms; inflected forms; possessives; contractions; base words. In addition, sight words were presented with each new lesson and were cumulative.

The curriculum for the second grade assumed the preceding skills and built upon them. The children were now taught decoding and word-meaning knowledge by learning to identify base words and affixes. They also learned to read multisyllable words. By the end of second grade, the curriculum materials consisted of fairly complex text written in a variety of genre—stories, poems, nonfiction, informative, and so on. The children were assumed to possess an extensive sight word store and to be able to use context and graphophonemic knowledge along with other word analysis skills to decode unfamiliar words. By the end of second grade, the children were assumed to be capable of reading independently from texts they had never heard before and to derive enjoyment and/or information from these texts.

The school district had recently adopted a "whole class" teaching philosophy.[10] This meant that progress was made through the curricular materials by everyone at the same time. The traditional "reading groups," based on ability, were no longer allowed, although individual teachers made varied attempts to "meet the needs" of the children who were behind the rest of the class and those who clearly needed more challenging material. In essence, though, the net effect of the "whole class" approach resembled that of a train moving inexorably forward with no stops. While some children became irritated with the sluggishness of the progress, others were trying desperately to hang on as the train hurtled perilously down an undeviating track.

Donny, however, was not even trying to hang on. He had been left at the station, wondering where he was and why he was there.

At the beginning of second grade, with the curriculum focused on the skills and assuming those concepts just described, Donny knew the following: that his name could be written, that print is "read" and not pictures, and that books could be "read" by looking at the pictures and producing one's own language to go with them. This was Donny's understanding. From the perspective of the curriculum, he did not know that letters have sounds, he did not know the difference between the instructional terms "spell" and "read," he did not know all of the letter names, and he did not know that one must match eye gaze to individual words in order to read. He did not even know what a "word" was.

During Donny's first year in the Literacy Center, he began to move forward, to develop as a reader/writer, to learn to read. But the train was down the track and almost out of sight by this time. Donny first learned that language can be represented with print, and he moved tentatively into an early understanding of the phonemic basis of written English through invented spelling, using letter names as a heuristic. At the same time he still had unstable word knowledge—he could not "remember" words he had learned from one day to the next—and he was unaware of the ways in which print functions in the world.

By the middle of this year, Donny had moved to a more consistent phonemic spelling of words and was beginning to be able to decode simple consonant-vowel-consonant words. His understanding that letters have an invariant order within words was still unstable, however. He soon was beginning to master decoding of consonant-vowel-consonant words and was consistently demonstrating eye-voice match when reading. He knew the concepts of "letter" and "word." He did not know the sounds associated with digraphs *(th, sh, wh),* and his knowledge of the short vowel sounds was unstable. He was still confusing some letter *names* with *sounds,* and he knew only three to five basic sight words.

By the end of his first year in the Center and his second-grade year at school, I could conclude that he now understood that print is used for the functions of written stories and personal narrative, letters and postcards, directions, and environmental signs. He still confused some letter names with sounds, had trouble with final consonant blends, could not remember the sounds associated with consonant digraphs, had trouble with r-controlled vowels *(car, fur)*, and was not consistently processing within words from left to right. He was able to read familiar text with some fluency and to read simple, unfamiliar text with a great deal of support.

Donny's second-grade teacher told Jenny that she would recommend retention. This was what Jenny had wanted for a year, now, and I concurred. Repeating second grade was the only chance Donny had to catch up to and board the train, given the mind-set and culture of the school district and its strict adherence to a preset curriculum with its carefully ordered scope and sequence. I only believed retention was useful, though, because it would allow him more time to work in the Literacy Center while, essentially, holding the curriculum still. Without this outside help, repeating the same curriculum would have been meaningless.

One More Year

Over the summer, although the Literacy Center was officially closed, I continued to meet with Donny as often as possible. These sessions took place at his home as well as in the Center. We continued with the same variety of activities, including focused phonics lessons. One ongoing literacy project became the center of our efforts. I felt that my "curriculum" for Donny could not continue to move forward until Donny consolidated the many literacy concepts he had tentatively acquired the previous year. The instability of his new knowledge was a clear indication that he did not totally control it. He needed to see words in meaningful text over and over again while he worked with the various graphophonemic principles and the order principle. He needed to *see* print as a code from the outside in and the inside out, from whole to part and part to whole, to grasp the essence of its form and function.

We decided to "make" a book. This came about as I reread one of Donny's favorite storybooks to him, *Where the Wild Things Are,* one day.[11] I commented that the wild things reminded me of Timmy, his younger brother. Donny grinned, and with eyes sparkling, suggested that I reread the book and substitute Timmy's name for Max. I agreed, and we partner-read the book again.[12] Capitalizing on Donny's interest in the book, I suggested that we rewrite the book with Timmy substituted for Max as the main character. Although we had composed several books previously from Donny's dictation, with each of us taking turns reading and spelling during the final production stage, this time I suggested typing the book in an attempt to alleviate the fatigue and strain these activities had brought about in the past. Donny agreed enthusiastically when he saw the typewriter and observed my demonstration of how it worked. A machine that printed letters! He had never seen one before.

My primary goal with this activity was to enable Donny to grasp the concepts of part to whole, letter to word, and invariant order through the manipulative activity of "making" each word, one letter at a time, on a machine. We usually devoted about half of each session to this project. We took turns; one person would read and dictate while the other would type. The reader would read an entire page of text, then go back and reread it sentence by sentence. At the end of each sentence, the reader would reread the sentence word by word, spelling each word letter by letter. The typist would find the letters and type, checking the paper for errors and rereading the text at the end of each sentence. When we finished, we cut the typescript into strips of text and pasted them onto photocopied pages of the pictures. Donny excelled at this phase of the production process. We bound the pages between pieces of heavy construction paper at front and at back, and Donny took it home to read to Timmy.

Within a few weeks, we had repeated this process with a simple version of *The Three Little Pigs*. During this second venture, I documented real progress in Donny's ability to spell by chunks of syllables or whole words, to name and identify correctly (find on the keyboard) all of the letters, and to hold several words in his consciousness as he typed. These abilities transferred to his reading also, as he read with increasing fluency, consistently processing left to right and acquiring an increasing store of automatically recognized words as whole chunks.

I also pushed Donny, during these summer sessions, to produce more of his own writing. One of the activities I used for this was to require him to keep a daily log of his activities in the center. I taped this to the wall so that we could refer to it over the sessions. A typical day's log looked like this (I provided the "starter" of *Today I*):

> Today I
> tipt n rad
> [typed and read]

I also included a journal-writing time in each session. For the first time, I demonstrated for him a type of "parallel writing" during which I would write in my own journal while he was writing in his. At the end of the time set aside for this, we would share what we had written by reading it aloud, if we wished (I always did). Donny enjoyed this variation on the "writin' time." Whenever I subsequently asked him if he would rather write together (with me scribing for him) or separately, he always chose parallel writing.

Donny's independent productions during these activities were sparse, however. He would often take up the entire allotted time "thinkin' what to write." As he thought—usually aloud—he found it difficult to avoid jumping up and running over to me to tell me his thoughts and stories. When I would send him back to his journal to write them down, he was largely at a loss. It seemed too hard to him, compared with the great facility with which he could "tell." Without the social context of other children writing and sharing, the incredible effort it took for him to form written versions of his thoughts was just not worth it to him.

We ended these summer sessions with a collection of books to be taken home, books written (and "published") by Donny as well as simple texts that Donny could read on his own.

Donny began school about a month before the Literacy Center, which operates on the university schedule, opened. Thus close to two months passed between our summer sessions and the fall ones. I heard from Jenny, though, about two weeks before the Center opened. She called me to report that, contrary to what we had heard in the spring, Donny had been promoted to third grade. She was beside herself with anger and worry. An intervention on my part resulted in a change of mind by the school, however, and Donny began his second pass through second grade and his second year in the Literacy Center.

Donny continued to progress, but slowly, during this year. He was now reading independently from books written for beginning readers. He was writing independently also, although this continued to present greater difficulties than did reading. I encouraged increased reading at home, requiring Donny to keep a reading chart recording at-home reading. This was something that was required of all children who attended the Literacy Center, and with Donny's newly acquired independence, he could now participate in this activity.

In addition to the self-directed reading and writing activities of Donny's first year in the Center, several new activities were embarked upon during this second year. These were motivated by the pressure I was feeling to "catch Donny up" to the school curriculum. I sensed that if he did not join the others on the train by the end of this year, he would be irretrievably lost to a world of remedial classes, increasing failure, and perhaps a fate similar to that of his parents.

Accordingly, I began to introduce Donny to more expository text. In the past, narrative had predominated in his reading and writing, which is typical of most beginning literacy programs. As learners advance in school they are increasingly required to learn from text, however, and this text is increasingly written in an expository style. It is on this switch from simple narrative to exposition that many children falter in their ability to perform in school.

Donny was in many ways a "natural" for receptivity to exposition. He was unusually curious about many things in the world: pine cones, dinosaurs, wars, cars, snakes. He asked questions and he hypothesized answers. He also possessed a surprising store of information. He knew about the controversy over the extinction of the dinosaurs; he knew the names of many types of animals and bugs; he knew about wars and could label fighter planes as well as make models of them; and he was familiar with many technical vocabulary words such as "excavate" and "prehistoric."

With this store of background knowledge and language, he should have been sufficiently motivated and prepared to read text for information.

I began our foray into information books by reading to him.[13] Often these events followed a question from Donny. He was fascinated by the many pictures that illustrated most of these texts. One of his favorite books to look at was about how things work, with pictures and text providing simple explanations of everyday items such as cranes, bulldozers, ice cream makers, and televisions. Over time, I encouraged Donny to do his own reading from expository texts. He could do this, at this point, only with heavy scaffolding from me. He surprised me with his ability to elaborate on the text orally, however, revealing his store of background knowledge.

It was during one of these events, as we read a book on dinosaurs, that I discovered the source of his vocabulary and concept knowledge. We were sitting in the kitchen of his home, and Jenny was alternating her time between listening to us and keeping Timmy occupied in the living room. As Donny was explaining to me one of the theories scientists hold about the extinction of dinosaurs, Jenny came up and began to contribute to the discussion. I asked Donny how he knew so much about this.

"Watch it on TV!" he chirped. "We got tapes on dinosaurs, 'n ever'thing."

Jenny confirmed this, and explained that Big Donny was very interested in many natural history and historical topics. Whenever a program was aired on television, he would record it on videotape to add to their library. The entire family had learned both content and language about a variety of topics as they repeatedly viewed these tapes.

Donny moved to an initial attempt at encoding written exposition when he asked to take part in a science activity being made available in the Literacy Center. A large poster taped to the wall explained the steps participants were to take to explore the concept of "Force." As Donny read these aloud, he decided to follow the instructions. The activity involved the children in exploring the concept of force and friction through several different experiments. With each one, the learner was to make and record a hypothesis in a research notebook. As the experiment proceeded, the observations were also recorded in the notebook. The hypothesis was then to be confirmed or altered to fit the observations. The culmination was the writing of a book on the topic that could teach others about the concept.

Donny greatly enjoyed the activities of dragging cartons alternately filled with books, pillows, or empty across carpets, tile, and grass. He made informed hypotheses and carefully recorded his observations. With reference to several published science books, he was able to produce one of his own on the topic of Force. All of the writing during this activity was heavily scaffolded by me. I scribed for him most of the time to relieve him of this task while he struggled to produce the language required. While I scribed, though, I involved him in spelling and punctuation decisions. In all, it was a thoroughly satisfying activity and one that engaged Donny throughout the days it took to complete it.

In addition to increased exposure to exposition, the second year in the Center brought more focus on Donny's homework. Although Donny's inability to do the work sent home during his first year was apparent and of great concern, I had concluded that the work sheets and assignments, focused on spelling and decoding, were too distant conceptually for Donny to benefit from help in doing them. But by now he controlled many of the concepts required for such work, and I was anxious for him to succeed in his classroom as soon as possible. Therefore some time was spent almost every session in at least going over the homework with Jenny and Donny and, at times, actually working through it with Donny.

The terrifying mismatch between the preset curriculum and Donny's conceptual understandings and skills, however, became immediately clear and continued through the end of the year. I documented various events as markers of the difficulties Donny faced in attempting to make sense of and utilize the formal literacy instruction he was receiving in school:

- At the beginning of this school year, Donny was assigned spelling and writing homework with "short" 'i' words. He could read only one word out of the twenty-five: *will.* He was totally confused regarding the directions.
- Also near the beginning of the year, Donny was given homework with simple sentences mimeographed on

a sheet of paper, on which he was to underline the 'predicate' and then the 'subject.' He had actually only begun to encode words in print in roughly sentence form and had no idea of the abstract concepts of 'predicate' and 'subject.'

- In late fall of this year, Donny had homework drilling on the 'th' and 'sh' digraphs. He said to me that 'sh' makes the /su/ sound. For the word *sheep,* I read with him very slowly, /shhh/ /ee:/ /p/, but he said /up/ for the /eep/ part. I did some double vowel rule work. Then he said that *teeth* says 't-u-eeeee-ch.' I took him to the board and tried to teach and sort out the two different digraphs. He had a very hard time with it. We then went back to the homework sheet and with a lot of scaffolding/teaching by me, he did it. But he could not handle at all the two syllable words like *finish.*
- This winter, Donny had a language arts sheet for homework that neither Jenny nor he could read. He was to put short sentences together with *because* (for example, *He ate dinner. He was hungry.*) On another sheet he was to circle the 'verbs' in sentences.
- This spring, Donny was assigned numerous practice sheets for the *California Achievement Test* which contained skills that were clearly beyond him.
- From a parent/teacher conference in March, I gathered more of these skill practice sheets and a *Weekly Reader* that Donny could read only with strong scaffolding.
- From his school book, Donny read a story that he had read (as a member of his class) in school. He needed strong scaffolding. Some words he got with clues, but the following I had to give: *could, season, player, needed,*

tryouts, sure, throw, we'll, since, swish, thump, sighed, sister, wait, each, wrote, asked, smiled, threw.

- Toward the end of this year, Donny had to learn to spell the months for a spelling test. At home, Jenny reported, he could only learn *May* and *June*. He wrote 'Septimbr.' When I tried to help him learn them in the Center, he tired quickly and engaged in numerous attempts to avoid focusing on the task. At one point, Donny, at my request, spelled them for his mom to write. He began 'o-c-t'; I asked him what he was spelling, and he said "August."

Despite my efforts and Donny's incredible conceptual growth, there was still no real place for him to connect with the curriculum at school.

During this second year in the Literacy Center, I continued focused instruction in decoding and phonics. Again, this work was always preceded and followed by the reading and writing of authentic text. Jenny soon joined our lessons in decoding, and the interactions between mother and son over literacy learning and events are described in Chapter 5.

Theory and Practice

Although my instructional approach to facilitating Donny's literacy development reflected many current beliefs about effective reading/writing instruction and diagnosis/evaluation,[14] my decisions and responses to Donny were primarily framed by my view of literacy as a cultural activity. While this frame is often implied and assumed by holistic, child-centered, developmentally based methodologies, it is seldom presented explicitly. Nor are its implications laid out and developed for learners from literacy cultures which differ from that assumed by the mainstream schools.

My stance as a teacher was thus that of a guide into the world of literate activity. I assumed that this was a new and unfamiliar world to Donny and so I described it and explained it as we went along. I pointed out print in his environment and talked about why and how people use it (for example, "So they know which door to go in to go to the bathroom"; "So you know that there is a telephone inside the booth"). I explained the ways in which written text must span time and space as we worked to compose both exposition and narrative (for example, the kite book and letters and postcards). I placed the crucial learning of the "inner workings" of print[15] (for example, phonics, concepts about print) within the contexts of authentic literacy events that were personally meaningful and functional to him (for example, "making" a book on the typewriter to read to Timmy). I provided him with opportunities to learn about the syntax and vocabulary of the various genres of written text by reading extensively to him and with him.

Using the frame of literacy as a cultural practice, I relied on my knowledge of the ways in which written language differs from oral in forms and functions to guide my responses to Donny's development—to guide my instructional moves. I did not assume that Donny's rich oral tradition and ability was sufficient to provide him with the base upon which to build reading and writing skills. Instead, I intentionally worked to move print in its various functions and forms into his life so that he, as a language learner, could acquire written language concepts from which he could productively interpret reading and writing instruction.

I did not assume, however, that simply "exposing" him to print and its functions would result in the same type and degree of knowledge acquired by children who grow up in rich literacy environments. I glossed this exposure with clear, direct, explicit explanations and instruction. Many, if not most, cultural practices are learned implicitly through participating within the culture. For those new to a culture, though, the implicit must be made explicit to the degree to which the new participant can appropriately interpret behaviors and ways of seeing that are unknown to him or her.

One cannot, of course, explicitly "teach" all there is to be learned about cultural practice, and this is not what I am advocating. When learners are having problems understanding, however, direct explanations and instruction are called for until the learner can begin to participate in the cultural practice more as an insider than an outsider. Reading and writing are cultural practices, and direct instruction is required for those experiencing problems with them. It is unfair and unethical to withhold insider information until children, or adults, "figure it out for themselves," as if they were insiders all along.[16]

5

In Her Own Words: Jenny

I had agreed to Jenny's request to attend the Literacy Center as a student without any real plan in mind for her instruction. She had anticipated that she could sit alongside Donny while I taught him and learn with him. Given Donny's developmental needs, however, this was not the best use of her time. Nor would it have worked, given Jenny's notions of what constituted appropriate instruction.

Throughout the two years Jenny and Donny attended the Literacy Center, Jenny struggled to understand the experiential, developmental approach to teaching and learning embraced by the Center. From Jenny's perspective, one was supposed to learn by working hard at assignments given by a teacher. Throughout, her recorded spontaneous comments and reactions reflect a belief that learning to read takes incredible effort and hard work. This work involves listening to a teacher tell you what the words are and practicing them until you know them. She also believed that if only someone would make her (and Donny) learn all the rules for reading words ("sounding out" rules), then she would be able to read.

The fact that she and Donny had been given this form of instruction without noticeable effect Jenny attributed to personal deficits. Donny was just "slow" and "lazy." She herself had been unable to learn because of her way of speaking.

"That's why it was a little hard for me startin' to like . . . sound my words out . . . 'cause I talk different . . . 'cause I'm you know . . . countrified. And my words don't come out the way they're supposed to."

At times I would invite Jenny to sit alongside while she listened to Donny read a familiar text or share a piece of writing. She found this hard to do, becoming irritated with his wiggling and tapping and his tendency to play with paper and markers as I read to him. "Pay attention!" she'd snap. "You ain't never gonna learn if you don't sit still and work!"

Jenny also believed that one needed specially written texts to learn to read from, texts like workbooks and work sheets. When she realized, for example, that the tapes I was sending home for Donny to listen to on a tape player were story tapes, she was surprised. "Are these the kind of tapes you mean? I though you meant *learnin'* tapes!"

All of this made it inadvisable for her to sit alongside Donny for the first year and a half. My challenge was to find a way for her to benefit from the Center, to help her reach her goal of being able to read well enough to do those things she wanted to do: read to her children; help Donny with his homework; read the environmental print around her; and read the notices from Donny's school.

My logistics problem, as I saw it, of maintaining a one-to-one relationship with Donny while still helping Jenny led me to suggest an activity which, from Jenny's perspective, was odd and absurd. After concluding that Jenny was accurate in her description of herself as a nonreader, I was faced with the problem with which many teachers of adults contend: materials. My theoretical and knowledge base as a teacher of reading and writing told me that Jenny needed to read meaningful, predictable text in order to begin to develop as a reader. But where to find such texts?

I strongly suspected that it was Jenny's stance as a nonreader that was primarily responsible for her inability to read. In other words, because she believed she could not read, she did not attempt to read anything—including print within her own world. Marie Clay[1] makes a strong case for the assertion that readers develop only as they come to control the various synergistic components of the system through their own efforts at figuring it out. Supported by informed interactions with a teacher, or guide, at the beginning, the learner develops a self-extending system—that is, the more a reader reads real text successfully, the better she will become at reading. The same may be said of writing and composing.

Many teachers of beginning reading understand that

the most predictable written text is that of one's own language. With young children, putting this idea into practice often entails a teacher's writing down the children's oral renderings to be read back by them.[2] Drawing on this principle, I suggested to Jenny that she begin writing in a journal so that I could transcribe it to provide her with a written text. This text would be the one from which she would learn to read; she would learn to read by reading her own words.

She was stunned! She was disbelieving. She felt sorry for me, believing I had failed to understand her reports of her illiteracy. "Why, I ain't never read my *own* words before!" she explained softly. "See, I cain't write!"

Doggedly pursuing my suggestion, I continued, "Well, I think you can write more than you think you can. The writing will come . . . as you start writing your own thoughts and your own feelings down, and not just copying somebody else's words."

Jenny shook her head back and forth slowly as she acknowledged, "That's all I ever really did was copy stuff, you know, from a book."

Focusing on her inability to spell, Jenny continued to try to convince me that she was not up to this task.

"See, I don't . . . the reason I blew up [I'm not sure what this referred to] was I couldn't spell stuff!" she insisted.

Her strength and determination to learn to read won the day, though, as she finally agreed to begin the arduous, and heretofore unthinkable, task of trying to record her thoughts and feelings on paper . . . *in her own words*. When she asked what to do about the words she could not spell, I advised her to spell them the way she heard them.

"Like how *I* hear it?" she repeated uncertainly.

"Of course," I replied. "How else could you do it?" She shook her head with foreboding.

In spite of her misgivings, Jenny acquiesced to my request: she wrote her own words for the first time in her life. She worked at a carrel in the Center, surrounded by six children and their tutors, while I attended to Donny. At times she would rise, stretch, and go out into the hall to smoke a cigarette. She would soon return and resume her task.

I checked back with her toward the end of the session. She had completed her first entry and I asked her to read it back to me. She read quietly but somewhat fluently—something she had never done before. She was, for the first time, reading meaning-laden language, not just separate words. She sounded like a real reader.

I typed her journal entry between this session and the next, spelling the words conventionally and inserting punctuation. When presented with her transformed writing, Jenny's eyes glowed with wonder and pride. She visibly suppressed any outward display of pleasure, though, true to her Appalachian sense of propriety which forbids one to "brag on" oneself. Instead she focused on her poor spelling, expressing amazement that I could read her writing. The concept that someone could read what she wrote was completely new to her. This first journal entry is displayed in Figure 3. My typed version read:

> Monday. I went to Ethel's to clean. The biggest mistake I made. She had me clean some in the house, and we went outside. I raked leaves the rest of the day. I filled up 9 garbage cans and about 4 big boxes and I don't know how many baskets of leaves. Then I went home and cleaned my house and gave the kids a bath. I took my bath and went to bed.

As Jenny read her transformed text to me, she was slightly less fluent than before but still read it as if it were language and not a collection of unrelated words. Again, she played down her accomplishment, protesting that she already knew what it said.

"But you didn't have it memorized, did you?" I pressed.

"No," she admitted, "I just sort of remembered what I wrote about."

"Well," I went on, trying to explain, "people who read *usually* have a good notion what it will be about. And they use those expectations to help them read the words."

"I didn't know that," she said, marveling.

The journal writing routine continued over the two years: Jenny recording one day, my typing the entry, and Jenny reading it back at the next session. The transformed texts were collected in a binder for her to read whenever she wished and to use for reference during her writing time. I would often see her flipping

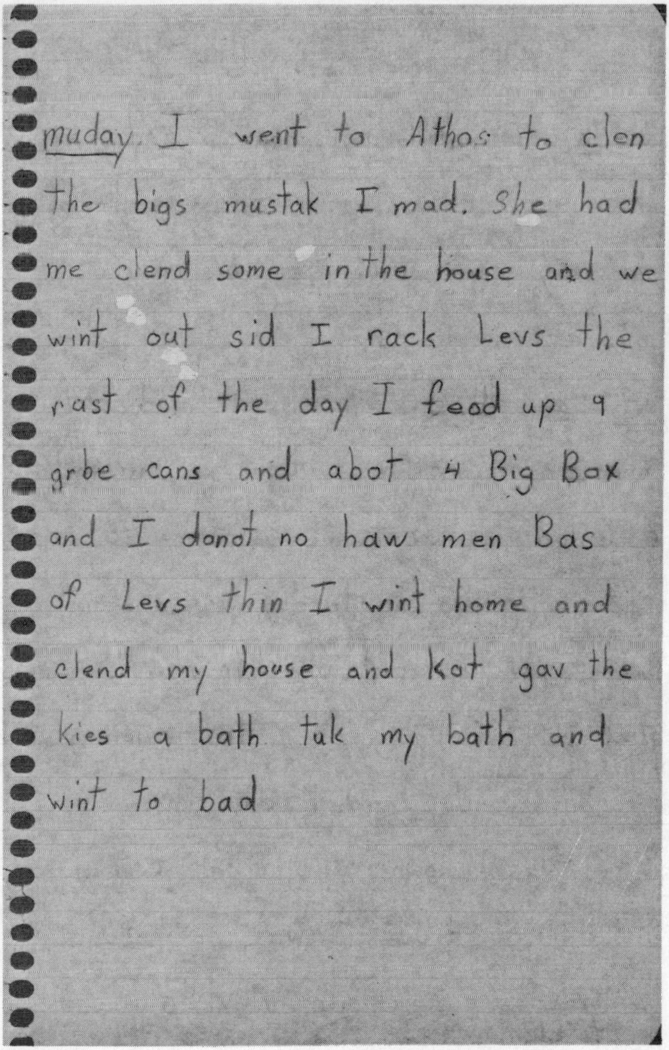

muday I went to Athos to clen
the bigs mustak I mad. She had
me clend some in the house and we
wint out sid I rack Levs the
rast of the day I feod up 9
grbe cans and abot 4 Big Box
and I donot no haw men Bas
of Levs thin I wint home and
clend my house and kot gav the
kies a bath tuk my bath and
wint to bad

Figure 3 A portion of Jenny's first journal cntry.

back through the pages of this collection, rereading and rethinking. Over time, she began to use these texts for spelling needs as she realized that these words of hers were written in conventional ways to be used over and over again.

As Jenny acquired a larger sight vocabulary and accumulated time reading real text for meaning, I began responding to her individual entries, providing her with her first meaningful text from an author other than herself. As I wrote for her to read, I was conscious of the need to keep the difficulty of the text within what Vygotsky calls the zone of proximal development.[3] This meant that it should be text that she could have produced, but with enough new, or challenging, material to stretch her and allow her to grow and develop.

My first written response to Jenny's writing followed a journal entry remarkable for it compositional unity and presence of tone and voice. This entry marked a developmental milestone for Jenny in terms of her writing. For the first time, she had shifted from a simple listing of a day's events to a struggle to compose a representation of a particular event. As this move occurred, her journal entries began to spill over from one session to another so that the unity of the composition spanned several entries. Her comments during and after each writing episode changed from the "I wrote everything I could think of" variety to statements like, "It's hard to say it so that it's like it really was."

In this particular journal entry, Jenny recounted the

terrifying night that the police broke into their apartment and arrested her husband for selling marijuana to friends, a fairly common practice in Big Donny and Jenny's Kentucky mountain region. The typed version of that entry and my response follow (the underlined words are those Jenny was unsure of and marked to ask me about).

April 5, 1990

Vicki, I hope you do not think I'm a bad person for what I'm going to tell you. Big Donny smokes pot, and he would sell some to his friends, and one night, the narcotic men came in. I was sleeping, and Donny and Timmy was sleeping, but Big Donny was awake. The men came running in the living room. That is where we sleep; the bedroom is too cold to sleep in. Right then the men hollered something. I do not know what they hollered. I cannot remember what they said, but I can remember hearing the guns click as they came running in. They told Big Donny to get up and go in the kitchen. Big Donny was sitting on the couch, watching TV. I was on the pallet. A woman told me to get up and come in the kitchen so I did, and I was so scared. That man was asking Big Donny where he had his pot at. Big Donny told him. While he was talking to me and Big Donny, the other men was tearing my house apart. There was nothing I could do but just sit at the kitchen table like they say. Big Donny had 3 bags of pot. I did not know how much pot he has. I do not pay any attention to how much pot he has because I do not ask him and he did not tell me nothing about it. I had told Big Donny many times to stop smoking pot, but he would not listen to me. So because of Big Donny's mistakes, I have to pay for it too because I live in the same place, and I know about him selling to his friends and him smoking pot. The law says you cannot do that. When we went to court, Big Donny got 3 to 6 months in jail. He had stayed in the Justice Center for 2 weeks, and his lawyer got the judge to send him to a drug center. I hope that it can help Big Donny stop smoking pot because if he don't, I will leave Big Donny. I love him, but I love my kids and I will not let that happen again because they can take my kids away from me. Just because I know about it, and I got 20 hours of working for the city and had to go to a drug and alcohol and got 5 years of probation for doing nothing but knowing what was going on. I do not smoke pot, and I do not drink, but they had made me go there. It was very embarrassing to me. And with Big Donny getting caught, he might see how wrong he is for doing what he was doing. I hope so anyway. That is all I can talk about right now and I hope you don't get mad at me.

April 23, 1990
Jenny, I am not mad at you, and I do not think you are a terrible person. I think this must have been a terrifying experience for you! When you wrote about how you could hear the guns click as the men rushed in, I could just feel how awful that must have been. I would have turned very cold, thinking that someone was going to shoot me and my kids. I really admire how hard you work to make things good for your family, especially for Donny and Timmy. If it is ok with you, I will try to write back to you in your journal from now on.

Jenny had already told this story to me in a whispered voice after abandoning her attempts to shield me from this part of her life. She and Donny had missed almost a month of sessions at the Center, and my attempts to contact her by phone had been unsatisfactory. When I finally did reach her, she had informed me that she could not bring Donny to the Center because one of their cars was not working and the van and the pickup were down home. It was only after I volunteered to pick them up at their home and bring them to the Center that Jenny revealed the extent of her difficulties and anxieties.

Big Donny's six-month incarceration and Jenny's resulting assumption of head of household responsibilities shaped our experiences together for many months to follow. It turned out that the police had confiscated two of their cars on the night of the arrest. Jenny had driven the pickup down home to James and Karen's to protect it from the police. Their cars were never returned. For a while, the family was under suspicion of theft after the police discovered dishes, silverware, and a boy's bicycle in the van. Jenny's explanation that these were items about to be transported down home in preparation for the (always) imminent move went unheard until the case was dropped for lack of evidence.

I thus began to transport them regularly to and from the Center, at times working with Donny at home. The times spent together in my car provided rich opportunities for sharing experiences and developing a deeper relationship.

Jenny's writings began to reflect her new circumstances. She described her frustration with the process of applying for food stamps and trying to convince "the lady" that she did not want welfare. Her need for a car of her own and for increased independence from helpful friends and family resonates through several of her entries, including one from early May:

> May 2, 1990
>
> Well, all of that is over now, so I hope we are getting along ok. Sometimes it is hard. Like when I just want to go somewhere, I can't. If I had a car of my own, I could go when I want to. I would like to take Timmy and Donny up at the park and feed the ducks. They would like that. And when I use other people's cars, I put gas in, and then when I need to use it again, there is 5 more dollars gone. If I had my own, I would have plenty of gas. The money I put in other cars, I would have gas all of the time. And if it wasn't for Vicki, Donny would be kicked out of [the Literacy Center]. She comes and picks us up. She is nice to us.

She also divulged her secret fear of storms and tornados as she described lying awake at night during a thunderstorm:

> May 21, 1990
>
> Timmy is playing with play dough and I'm going to get a book. But a woman come out so that I can go in and do some work. Well I don't know what to write about. I'm going to go to work tomorrow if it don't rain. She wants me for outside work. Big Donny needs money and we need money, but we

can get by without money as long as we have food. We are doing good. If I can work for them women, I will send Big Donny the money, all but 10 dollars I give to my Mom. $5 is for gas and $5 is for her. She watches Timmy. When I get my welfare check, if I have some money left I'm going to get someone to take me to the store you was talking about for learning stuff for Donny and Timmy. It is so hard sometimes. Like last night, it was storming so hard I was a little scared. I don't tell no one that I'm afraid of storms. I'm not so much afraid of storms as I am of tornados.

I was listening to Little Red Riding Hood, and I like it. When I get good like they do on reading books, I will like it a lot. I'm reading a lot more than I thought I could. I surprise myself; like sometimes I will look at a paper, and I'll try to read it. Sometimes I can read what it says. Not all of the time, but more than I could before. It makes me feel good because I'm getting better. I'm going to work for the 85 year old woman tomorrow. I wonder what my day will be like. I hope she stays in her room because I don't want her coming in where I'm cleaning at. I will let you know what happens tomorrow. I hope that I have a good day.

Jenny engaged in other activities in the Literacy Center that helped her develop as a reader. The most effective one was that of listening to children's books on tape.

The challenge to educators of adults—that of finding appropriate materials—was partly circumvented by the happy coincidence of one of Jenny's reasons for wanting to learn to read and the somewhat simplified nature of books written for children to hear read aloud. Jenny had been told that parents should read to their children to help ensure their success in school. She was extremely frustrated by her inability to do this, dismayed when she had to disappoint Donny and Timmy whenever they asked her to read one of the children's books she had collected.

Tapping into this need, I suggested that she choose children's books in the Center to listen to on tape. She was to follow along with the print as the narrator read. When she felt sufficiently familiar with the book, she could take it home to read to the boys. I also provided books and tapes for her to take home to listen to on Donny's stuffed bear toy, which contained an embedded tape player (she refused my offer of a tape recorder, explaining that they had one in the toy).

Occasionally, Jenny would spend long stretches of time listening to books over and over again. When she felt ready, she would attempt to read the text on her own. She would often then return to the tape to master the few words she had missed and to listen again to the intonation and phrasing of the narrator. She mastered several children's classics in this manner, which she then read and reread to Donny and Timmy. As time went on, Jenny was able to "work out" simple children's books on her own without first hearing them on tape. She would practice these over time until she felt ready to read them to the boys.

By the end of the first year, Jenny had begun to read some of the environmental print around her. I discovered this the day I came upon her in the hallway before a session, attempting to make sense of one of the many notices posted on the walls of the university building. As she reread a notice aloud to ask me about it, she suddenly stopped. "Sometimes I surprise myself," she said, grinning. "I didn't know I could read this good!"

Although I worked with Donny over the summer both at home and at the Center, Jenny did not take part in these lessons. She remained at home with Timmy, focusing on her daily chores and summer activities for the children. When she began attending the Center again the following September, she picked up with her journal, rereading the previous year's entries with fluency and pleasure, often chuckling over the many trials and tribulations she had described.

I saw less of Jenny, as a student, during this second year. When she did attend the Center, she usually wrote in her journal, listened to books on tape, and browsed for books to take home. Some of the books were for the boys to hear, and others were informational books for Jenny herself. For a time, she was particularly interested in learning as much as she could about snakes, particularly those prevalent in the region down home. She reported that relatives had warned her of the poisonous snakes in the woods and hollers, and Jenny wanted to prepare the boys for the time they moved permanently to the area. I sometimes read with her from different sources in the Center and helped her select appropriate books for her to take home. She found it extremely difficult, though, to retrieve enough information from these books to satisfy her, so this functional use of print for her was only marginally achieved.

During this year, Jenny and Donny joined forces for some of their activities in the Center. Donny began spontaneously sharing his journal stories with his mother as he observed her reading more and more on her own. Jenny joined us sometimes when I would read to Donny and participated in partner reading with us. During these events, Donny would engage with the task to a greater extent than I had previously observed when he worked with me alone. As his mother read, either from his journal or from a book we were reading, he would intently follow along, offering encouragement when she faltered and providing help when he sensed she needed it. I could sense an underlying anxiety in his attention to his mother during these sessions, as he would often rush to provide her with a word or to correct her reading. His Appalachian pride needed to protect his mother from embarrassment and shame, although Jenny was unusually open about her difficulties with reading and writing.

Similar interactions prevailed during the times Jenny would join Donny in phonics work. This type of instruction fit Jenny's schema for "real" reading instruction, and she asked if she could join us about halfway through the year. Phonics lessons were fraught with potential hazards for Jenny. She already believed that the reason she could not "sound words out" was because she spoke a dialect that was "wrong." She concentrated intently on pronouncing the words in the lessons, and was tentative in her responses. Donny often assumed a parental stance while she did this, coaching her, assuring her she could do it, and praising her when she was successful.

Soon, however , Jenny was successfully applying the strategies I stressed for using phonics knowledge while reading. I told her that good readers use phonics to get close to what the word might be. No one *speaks* exactly the way the phonics lessons reflect the sound/letter system. It doesn't matter *how you say it.* It only matters that you can recognize the word and that you can spell it accurately. Therefore, when the word is spelled 'r-a-w,' it should signal to her that the word is 'rawr' in her dialect. Good readers always use context to confirm the identity of a word: Does it sound right (like language)? Does it make sense? If not, good readers go back and self correct until it does.

This information was completely new for Jenny. But because she had experienced so much progress already, she quickly trusted this advice enough to apply it when reading text. Success followed, and she had another strategy for reading print.

First Visit to the Library

The year ended for Donny and Jenny with a long-planned trip together to the city library. The previous year, Jenny had summoned me over to her in the Literacy Center.

"A library?" she asked. "Is that its name? A friend of mine was tellin' me 'bout this big building that has lots of books in it? She says people can go there and get books. You know, it wouldn't cost you nothin'. Do you know anything about this?"

As other tutors discreetly glanced over at us in amazement, I replied that, yes, I did know about libraries. Yes, they do have lots of books, and people can borrow books for free if they promise to return them.

Jenny wanted to go to a library to get some books that she and Donny could read. I explained about the branch libraries, but concluded that she was probably closer to the main one downtown.

"I don't know nothin' about goin' downtown, you know, but I could find it. I know where I'm at when I'm downtown but I get lost down there."

I remarked that she could take a bus, but Jenny explained that she never rides the bus. She could not read the signs or the schedules. Donny volunteered that *he* knew how to ride a bus and thus could help her, but Jenny dismissed this with "A school bus!"

Jenny's plan to visit the library was interrupted for over a year by such real-life obstacles as illness, visits down home, lack of a car, and so on. As the second year of our sessions neared an end and I knew I would be moving to another city, I felt pressed to facilitate Jenny and Donny's continued reading as much as possible. Therefore I arranged with Jenny to accompany her and Donny to the downtown library.

I picked Jenny and the two boys up at their home one weekday afternoon. Timmy, who was an extremely active and noisy child, had been forewarned about appropriate behavior for a library ("I seen people go to a library on TV and I know you gotta whisper!"

reported Jenny). Both of the boys were shiny clean with their hair still wet from washing and combing. Jenny had donned clean, pressed jeans and t-shirt.

As we maneuvered the city streets between their home and the library, Jenny called out landmarks to herself, explaining that she needed to remember how to get there after I left town. Pushing her to abandon her old nonliterate habits, I pointed out the street names on poles. When she looked tentatively up at them, she read them correctly.

I parked the car about a half block from the front entrance to the library, and we climbed out with anticipation and excitement running high. Intent on focusing Jenny and Donny on the environmental print that would help them negotiate their activities, I pointed Jenny in the direction of the big sign at the end of the block on a large black marble stand and asked her if she could read it. She spelled out *P-u-b-l-i-c* and Donny read the whole thing quickly before she could. "Public Library!" She grinned and tousled his hair as she kidded, "Well, *excuse me!*"

After we entered the library, I told them that we had to find the children's section and walked over to the directory that displayed a list of the different areas. I asked Donny and Jenny if they could find the word *Children* on the list. Jenny cautioned Donny not to tell when he found it (because she wanted to find it too), but he quickly identified the word and pointed it out.

The children's department was on the second floor, so we headed toward the stairs. As we passed the Information Desk, I turned Donny around and asked if he could read the big sign over the desk. He read the first syllable and then pronounced, "Information!" I said that was correct and asked him what we would go to that desk for. He provided several examples, indicating we would go there if we needed to find out things about the library.

I then spotted the "Lending and Registration" sign, so we walked over to obtain library cards. One of the two well-dressed women behind the desk approached us. I announced that Donny needed a library card and so did Mrs. Browning. She replied that Donny would need to ask for his application form in the Children's Department, and handed Jenny hers. We moved toward the end of the long, curved desk to fill it out. I held back, and Jenny read the directions on the form: "Date of Birth." "Social Security Number." (She hesitated on this one, but worked it out independently.) "Address." And so on.

I read to her the paragraph which said that she agreed to abide by the rules and regulations of the library and to pay any fines owed. She asked what that meant, "You have to pay for the book?" I explained that if she did not turn it in on the date that it was due, then there would be a fine for each day it was late. And if the book were lost, then she would have to pay for the book. She nodded in agreement, indicating that she understood and that it seemed fair. She filled the application out, and a temporary card was printed for her.

We then ascended the stairs to the Children's Department. I went with Donny to choose books from the Easy Readers section. On the way down to the library, he had announced that he wanted some discovery books, and he restated this now. "You know, like discovering hidden treasure or about things in the water!" He found one on totem poles, and I found some on sharks and other fish. Together we picked out several story books.

Jenny chose a few books for Timmy that she thought she could read. Timmy picked a book with a "neat" picture of a turtle on the front. As we sat around a table, looking through the books we were thinking of taking, Donny argued for several books that he clearly could not read. Jenny stated unequivocally, "We don't *need* any more books we *can't* read! We got a whole house full of those! We need books we *can* read!"

We next asked for the application form for Donny's library card. He filled out the front of the form, with my coaching on such tasks as writing the date—"Is it 91 or 19?"—using a dash (which he first put as a comma), which way a capital 'L' goes, and how to write a lower-case 'l'. Authentic literacy tasks such as this one often reveal the extent to which skills learned in isolation generalize to life. Jenny, as instructed, filled out the back of the card with a mixture of cursive writing and printing.

Both to fulfill my own needs and to model literate behavior, I led the group down one level to the Adult Fiction section where I chose two books for myself. Donny noted the sign over the books I was looking at and asked, "Vicki, where are the father's books?" At my questioning look, he pointed to the sign that said

Mysteries and explained, "These are the Mother's; where are the Father's?" I explained that the sign said *Mysteries,* and that I liked to read mysteries, myself.

At the main registration desk again, we delivered the form for Donny's card to the same lady who had helped us before. There were some tense moments when she took one look at the back of the form and, looking at me, announced with some irritation that *the mother* was to have filled in this side. I replied that I was not the mother and indicated Jenny. She looked again at the back of the form, and then, showing it to me and Jenny, challenged, "*The mother* did this?!" When we replied affirmatively, she shrugged, rolled her eyes, and began punching the information into the computer.

The computer indicated that Donny had already been issued a card through another branch! Jenny said, "No; he couldn't have. I never took him to no library. This is the first time I ever set foot in one of these libraries!" Sorting out the confusion, I turned to Donny, who recalled going to a library with his class where they had all filled out cards. Jenny denied ever receiving one in the mail. I reminded her to look for the ones she had just applied for when the mail came in the future.

Turning now to the "Return and Cashier" desk, I turned in several books I had brought with me. I pointed the sign out to Donny and Jenny and explained that it indicated where they were to return their books and pay any fines. Jenny asked me how she would know when the book was due. I told her that they stamped a date on the book when you checked it out; I would show her when we checked out the books we had chosen.

Accordingly, we crossed to the check-out desk, controlled with a turnstile and magnetic reader device. I checked my books out first, followed by Donny and then Jenny. As Jenny was handed back her books, she asked the clerk how long she could have them. "Three weeks."

"O.K., Vicki. Show me where it says that," Jenny turned to me as she emerged from the turnstile. I pulled the card out of one of her books and pointed out that the latest date stamped on it was the due date. She declared that they could have it back by then because they were leaving for down home right after that. I assured her that I was planning to return with them before that date, anyway. Jenny responded in surprise, "You mean you can go there *any*time?" I said yes, and pointed out the hours during which the library was open, printed on the front door.

Progress toward Literacy

Although my observations of Donny and Jenny convinced me that they both had become readers and writers where once they were not, I sought to measure their progress, especially Jenny's, in more precise ways. I was particularly eager to examine her writings to look for growth, for several reasons. First, writing was the primary route I had chosen for her literacy growth. Second, she had never before encoded her own language—her own words—and I wanted to explore the benefit, if any, of this. I was juxtaposing this exploratory, experiential learning activity with the more artificial ones she encountered in elementary and adult schools.

I conducted this analysis[4] on a subsample of all of the writing samples I had saved over the course of the two years and the first letter she sent me after I had moved out of town (a portion of which is reproduced in Figure 4). In response to a letter sent Jenny from my new home, asking about how she and her family were doing and telling her about my new house and job, she wrote:

September

Hi Vicki
How are you doing. I hop you are doing good. if you take a pecher of your new home and send it to us. and when I get Donny and Timmy pecher taking I will geve you one. Sometimes at nit when it's to quiet it can be hord to get some sleep. when we go to Ky at nit it's hord for me to sleep it's to quiet ther. Is the peopl ther nice or not. Im shor you can set up a nice Literacy Center for the kids. I hope you can read what Im writeing. I got the word writeing off of Donny Spelling Book. No one has called me yet. Donny says that he like the new school. I have met his techer two times. Donny had to say avfter school. he didnot do his work and was toking. I had to go and pike hem up. and I thenk she is a grrach. and for Timmy he don't like school. he ses that he can't tolk when he wuns to. Timmy can tolk two much. he has met some new firends. he likes that but he

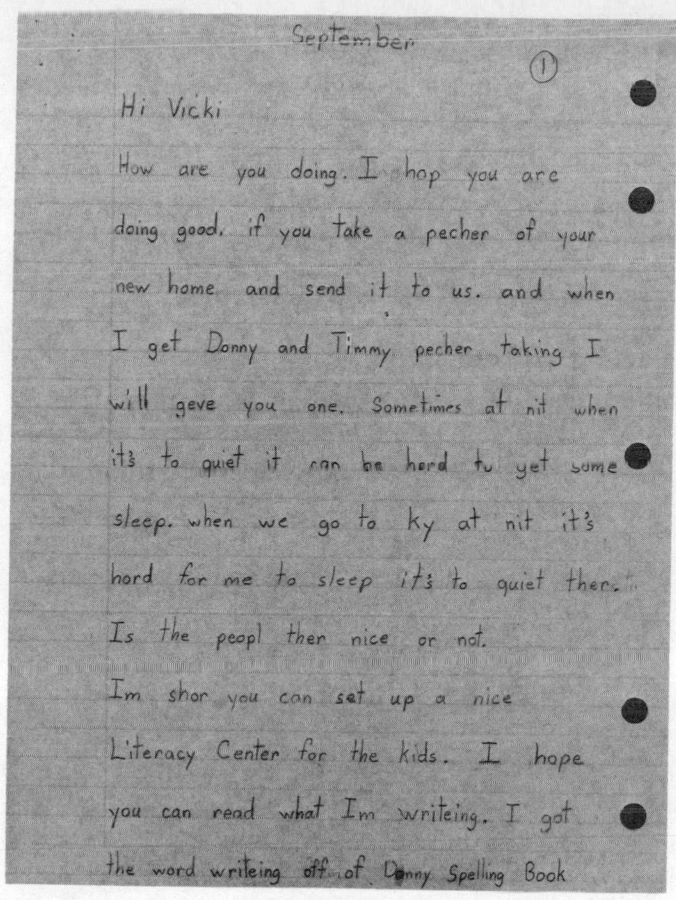

September

1

Hi Vicki

How are you doing. I hop you are doing good. if you take a pecher of your new home and send it to us. and when I get Donny and Timmy pecher taking I will geve you one. Sometimes at nit when it's to quiet it can be hord to get some sleep. when we go to ky at nit it's hord for me to sleep it's to quiet ther. Is the peopl ther nice or not.

Im shor you can set up a nice Literacy Center for the kids. I hope you can read what Im writeing. I got the word writeing off of Donny Spelling Book

Figure 4 A portion of Jenny's first letter to me after I had moved.

will be ok. The weather is nice it's not to hot and not to cold. I like it the way it is. the days weather was 67 to nit it's 30 something. is your weather nice. I have 5 women that I work for. I have one on friday and one on monday. and the uthers call me when thay ned me. when I was working for Terry the woman nix door saw me clening the windows and she ask me if that is all I do is windows I sad no I do ine kid of clening and so she ask me to clen for her on mondays or fridays I told her mondays. wold be good for me and that is how I got her. and big Donny has got his car runing agen. Now I have a car to drive. I go to my school naw. Some weeks it can be hrd. to work, and go to school and clen my on house. but days keep on going by thay dont stop. that is how I get by. I ges.

Your friend Jenny

Progress toward Conventional Writing

One can see by comparing the content and the form of the writing in Figure 2 and that in her letter that Jenny's writing moved from very nonconventional to close to conventional text. I documented this on several different levels.

First, because Jenny herself equated her inability to write to her inability to spell, I analyzed her spellings to check the impression that she became increasingly more accurate as she continued to write and then to read first her own writing, and later mine.

To analyze for an increase in accuracy from beginning to end, I averaged the percentage of words per journal (or letter) entry spelled conventionally for the first and last three entries, which included the letter. There was a 24 percent increase in words spelled accurately from the time she was convinced to encode text for the first time in her life to the end of the study period.

A more qualitative look at her move toward accurate spelling also reveals a move, or process. First, the words spelled correctly over the course of the entries reveal an increased complexity in the words she can spell.

Second, by examining words that Jenny initially misspelled but eventually encoded correctly, one can see evidence of a process of increasingly closer approximation to the conventional. A list of those words, with her initial spellings in the order in which they appeared over time in her writing, can be seen in Table 1. A list of words that she never spells correctly, but that all show a move toward convention over time, can be seen in Table 2.

This analysis confirmed for me that as Jenny encoded her own words, read them in standard form, and then read my words to her, she moved slowly but inexorably toward conventional control of written text.

I next looked at appropriate use of punctuation, a skill area she had repeatedly encountered in instruction during her first seven years in school and her four years in adult education classes. I again used the first and last three journal entries. I found that during the two-year period, she moved from the virtual absence

Table 1 Words that Jenny eventually spelled correctly over a two-year course of writing entries

Word	Previous spellings in order of appearance	Word	Previous spellings in order of appearance
Monday	Muday	them	tem, thm, thim
went	wint, wit, wnt, wint	keep	kep
about	abot, abad	when	win, wen, whin, wen
kids	kies, kis, keds	windows	windos
friend	frind, firend	school	sowl, sol, sool
her	hir, hr	did	ded
told	tod	spelling	saleing
called	cold	asking	asting
think	thek	pray	pra
look	luk	read	red

(8 percent) of punctuation to a near standard use of periods (94 percent used appropriately). In the first three entries, she used no commas at all; in the last three she indicated a sense of the need for a comma by using three periods where commas should go. Two of the periods used appropriately in the letter to indicate the end of a complete sentence should have been question marks. Periods were the only punctuation marks used in all of her writing entries.

Given Jenny's ascription of her nonliterate status to her "countrified words," which in her eyes—and, I

Table 2 Words that moved toward standard spelling over time in Jenny's writing

Successive spellings moving toward standard	Word
Dabc, Dabbc	Debbie
winday, winsday	Wednesday
trsday, tusday	Tuesday
teshr, tchr, techer	teacher
becs, becols, be calls, becols	because
Juhov, Juhova	Jehovah
rember, remmber	remember
srod, stred, strd, storded	started
ces, sens	since
qelt, qwelt	quilt
pepol, peopl	people

suspect, the eyes of more than one of her former teachers—prevented her from learning to sound out words, I decided to look at all of her misspellings for (1) an indication of phonemic awareness and (2) the influence of her dialect on her spellings. Phonemic awareness is the knowledge that the English language can be perceived at the level of the phoneme, roughly a letter-to-sound match. M. J. Adams (1990) has synthesized a vast amount of research indicating that learners must possess this knowledge in order to become fluent readers. Much of this research points out that many poor readers do not have this knowledge. Without it, a reader cannot "sound out" words in print, the skill Jenny reported she was unable to master.

One way of measuring the extent of phonemic

Table 3 Selection of Jenny's spellings in which every phoneme was represented graphically (total = 90 percent)

Jenny's spelling	Standard spelling
mustak	mistake
out sid	outside
Levs	leaves
tuk	took
min	mine
clening	cleaning
awr	hour
triing	trying
papr	paper
rit	right
muvd	moved

Table 4 Selection of Jenny's spellings that did not have every phoneme represented graphically (total = 10 percent)

Jenny's spelling	Standard spelling
Muday	Monday
grbe	garbage
Box	boxes
Bas	baskets
kied	kids
cled	cleaned

awareness is to examine invented, or creative, spellings. If individual phonemes are represented in regular ways, then it can be said that the speller is aware of the phonemic basis of English spelling. When I examined Jenny's misspellings for phonemic representation, I found that 90 percent of them had every phoneme represented. A sample appears in Table 3. The

Table 5 Selection of Jenny's spellings that reflected her Appalachian dialect (total = 33 percent)

Jenny's spelling	Standard spelling
Athos	Ethel's
mustak	mistake
rast	rest
masing	messing
haf	have
thin	then
ho	whole
famlee	family
fir	far
thar	there
war	where
sterl	still
worsh	wash
dines	dentist
har	hair

few inventively spelled words that did not have all of the phonemes represented each contained over half of them, as illustrated in Table 4.

When I next looked at her misspellings for dialect influence, I found that exactly one-third of them reflected her phonological system.[5] A selection of these spellings appears in Table 5. Jenny was thus very good at encoding language at the phonemic level as she heard it.

Progress toward Functional Reading

In terms of reading progress over this two-year period, Jenny moved from the level of a total nonreader to that of functional reading. Soon after she began to read my responses to her in her journals, I observed her attempting to read environmental print for the first time. She also began to puzzle out more and more of the notices that Donny brought home from school. I was soon able to leave her notes to which I knew she could read and respond. Finally, the episode of our first exchange of letters after I had moved was quite revealing of her increased functional literacy. It was a clear mark of progress that Jenny even spotted my letter to her in the mail, in contrast to my postcards from England, which had gone unnoticed, two years earlier. She was able to read my letter and write one of her own in response. I had included a stamped self-addressed envelope to facilitate this.

Theory and Practice

Again, as with Donny, my instructional approach to Jenny was framed by my view of literacy as a cultural activity. Jenny and Donny both had begun moving toward full literacy. I believe this was made possible because for the first time they were able to connect their lives with the world of print. Through the activities and environment fostered in the Literacy Center, and with me as a coach and a guide into the world of print, they saw print phenomenologically for the first time—encoding their world, signifying for them.

Jenny's biggest conceptual gain was her shift from viewing reading and writing as the identification and reproduction of individual words to an understanding that print encodes language. In order for her to do this, she had to dive into the print and use it, that is, read and write it. She did this through her journal writing and her reading of children's books. With both of these, she needed the scaffolding I provided for the journal writing and which the audiotapes provided for the children's book reading.

I believe that Jenny was only able to achieve this conceptual shift, which allowed her to begin to learn to read and write, because she was encouraged to read and write for her own, authentic purposes and with her own words. Once she had made this key conceptual move to understanding reading and writing as language use, she could move from her personal language base to an ever-expanding acquisition of other forms of written language, with their different vocabulary, syntax, and ways of saying.

Implicit in my decision to type Jenny's journal writings in conventional form, with all of the words spelled correctly and with appropriate punctuation, was my theory of the processes involved in the development of a reader from "beginning" to independent. It is the repeated processing of printed words during actual reading that enables readers to move to a level of automaticity of word recognition.[6]

Not until readers have acquired a large store of automatically recognized words in memory can they devote full cognitive attention to the comprehension processes needed to read fluently for meaning. This explains the phenomena of "the more you read, the better you read." My goal as a reading teacher has always been to help learners reach the level of development where they can read new text independently. From this point, I believe, the most effective "reading instruction" is composed for the most part of encouraging and facilitating volume reading by the learner for personally meaningful reasons.

For these reasons, beginning readers should not repeatedly "read" unconventional spellings and punctuation. This practice will neither aid their automatic recognition of words nor help them begin to gain an intuitive feel for conventional spelling patterns or written punctuation conventions. This does not mean that encouraging invented spelling is wrong; many good theoretical reasons exist for this practice, as we saw in Chapter 4. Rather, the "published" writing read by those learning to read and write needs to be in conventional form to provide the "convention" toward which the learner is moving.

Jenny learned to read and write by doing so for her own personal needs and purposes. In the process, I structured the reading and writing in ways that allowed her to connect with the world of print through her own "ways of saying" and to begin to acquire the conventional forms necessary for her full participation in a literate world.

6

Print Enters the World of Donny and Jenny

We have seen how the extent to which Donny and Timmy were able to build important concepts about written language was severely constrained by the relatively few functions for print in their home. I concluded that print did not signify for Donny and Timmy; it did not code their world; it did not mediate their lives. After almost two years of experiences with functional literacy events supplemented by direct explanation, however, the situation began to change.

One evening in late May of the second year, Jenny described the following scene to me when I asked if Donny was reading at home:

> Timmy surprises me! You should see! Donny, he'll read the Dinosaur book. O.K., Timmy likes the Dinosaur book; Donny read it to him last night. And I told Donny, like take your finger and go across as you read it so's Timmy will do it. And you know them little books we get from you? It's like so many

> pages and they're real easy. Timmy could read! I don't know if you could say he could *read.* He just memorized the words. But Donny would read to him, and he [Timmy] would read to Big Donny.

Print had entered Jenny's home. Print had entered Jenny's home in the sense meant by those who study and describe emergent literacy: print was being *used* by relevant members of the home and this use was a social one, by virtue of the social nature of families. Children, therefore, as participating members in this culture of the home, observed and participated in all of the different "ways of being" associated with uses of print.

Actually, Jenny was the first member of the family to bring print into their world. For her, a personally motivated need to write arose after Big Donny was sent to prison for six months. I had introduced to Jenny the basic conceptual notion that she could express herself on the personal level—use her own words—through print. By the time of Big Donny's arrest, she had learned through experience in the Literacy Center that she could write and that someone else could read it—and read her. Therefore, when Big Donny was arrested and sent away from the family, it *occurred* to her to attempt to maintain her relationship with him through the use of written language.

Of course writing was not the primary avenue of communication between Big Donny and Jenny. She, and often the boys, visited him weekly on Sundays. She would borrow her mother's car for the two-hour trip to the prison. During these visits, they would exchange news, and Donny and Timmy would sit on their Dad's lap and tell stories and tease. Messages from relatives down home were exchanged, and Jenny and Big Donny would discuss the future in terms of Big Donny's practice of marijuana smoking. Jenny, fearing that her children would be taken from her, was anxious to ensure that the police not enter their lives again in this way. Through regular and frequent visits, the family was thus able to maintain their relationships in face-to-face, orally mediated, encounters.

Jenny, though, was painfully lonely during the week. Her mother slept at her house many nights to help alleviate her loneliness and anxiety. Yet there were myriad thoughts and emotions that Jenny could share only with her husband and that occurred spontaneously during her day-to-day life. She wanted to tell him about the funny comment Donny had made, or the latest misadventure to befall Timmy. She wanted to report on the new housecleaning job she had acquired. She wanted to tell him that she loved him and missed him desperately. Jenny tried calling friends to see if they could stop by and write for her. When they failed to appear, she did not want to call and "bother" them again.

"So I tried writin' by myself. You know, like I write in here. Write it my own way—just the way I hear it."

When a friend would come by, Jenny would ask her to "fix" her letter to send. Jenny worried that without this final help, no one would be able to read it at the prison; because Big Donny could not read, a guard would have to read everything sent to him, and Jenny was skeptical about the guard's ability to read her writing like I did.

Donny picked up on this use of print, and decided

to write his own letter to his dad. Donny too missed his father terribly. During this time, he gravitated toward books that told stories of dads playing with their children and taking care of them. One of his favorite books, which he read over and over again, included a key scene in which the father carries his sleeping son up the stairs and tucks him in bed. As Donny read this part, his usually bright demeanor would fade and tears would fill his eyes. One of his most successful writing experiences around this time was a play he decided to write in which a dad carries his son upstairs to bed and defends him against the ghost waiting for him in the darkened bedroom.

A communicative need for print emerged, however, the day he surprised me by parking himself at the writing table when he first entered the Center. He announced that he was going to "write notes."

"Write notes? O.K. Who would you like to write a note to? Who do you need to tell something to?" I responded.

"My dad."

I pointed out the choices of stationery and envelopes available in the writing area, and he chose his favorite colors, green and yellow. He proceeded to print and soon asked me how to spell *like.* After I spelled it for him, he read to me:

"Do you like it?"

I looked at his letter and saw he had first written "I love you." I prodded, "What is it that he likes? This? When you say, 'I love you,' is that what you mean by, 'Do you like it'?"

"No. Does he like it there? He'll say, 'No.' 'n'-'o'."

"O.K. So then what would you say?" I continue.

" 'Did you break any dishes?' 'Cuz he washes dishes."

As Donny proceeded through his short letter to his dad, I provided spelling when asked and helped with formulating language that could be understood by his father who would not be able to question and negotiate meaning with Donny when he received it—as in an oral situation. When Donny indicated that he was finished, I asked, "Do you want to sign it so he knows who it's from?"

"How do you sign it?"

"Say, 'Love, Donny' at the very bottom so he knows it's the end," I directed.

As he placed the letter in the envelope, he asked what side to put "that stamp."

I showed him which side was the front and where the stamp would go. He picked up the scissors and began to cut slashes into the side of the envelope.

"What are you doing, Donny?" I said, quickly intervening. "Why are you cutting the envelope?"

"So he's know it's from me!"

I explained to him that an alternative to this was to sign his name up in the corner. "Whenever someone sends a letter, that's where they sign their name." We finished the letter writing event as I helped him address the letter. I told him I would mail it for him.

Jenny and Donny were both bringing books into their home soon after beginning at the Center. Jenny brought the books she had learned in the Center, with their accompanying tapes, and read them to the boys. She also brought home tapes to listen to on Donny's teddy bear tape player. She and the boys would listen together as they turned the pages of the taped books.

Donny began bringing books home to read soon after Jenny did. These were both published simple, predictable books Donny could read on his own and books he had dictated himself and bound with construction paper. At first these texts languished unread at home, as Donny quickly forgot about them when he reentered his familiar routines of rough and tumble play and television watching with his little brother. But after many months of concept building and experience in reading and writing meaningful texts, Donny began to include the books he brought home in his shared life with his family.

One late summer afternoon, as I climbed down the stairway from their flat into the backyard, I came across Big Donny, recently released from jail, holding Timmy in his lap as Donny read to both of them from a book he had mastered in the Literacy Center. As he read from *Where the Wild Things Are,*[1] I repeated my comment to Big Donny that Timmy reminded Donny and me of the "wild things" described by Sendak. Big Donny smiled gently and hugged Timmy closer while Timmy grinned delightedly and let out a BIG ROAR! I turned for one last look as I drove away and saw Donny finishing his reading as his father and younger brother looked on intently.

Soon, the books heretofore stored in cardboard boxes were moved to bedroom library shelves fashioned from orange crates. Both Donny and Timmy knew most of the books, and each had his favorites. At the time of one of my visits during the fall of the second year, Donny preferred the books on dinosaurs, while Timmy always chose a particular alphabet book.

Also during this second year of our relationship, the ubiquitous printed notices sent home by Donny's school became noticed and recognizable. For the first year and a half, Jenny always arrived at the Literacy Center with homework and notes from Donny's school for me to read to her. I served, during that time, as another friend who could be called upon to translate between her and the world of print. Nevertheless, much of what was sent to her in printed form was never available to her, either because she had no one to read it for her or because she simply did not attend to it. Over time, though, Jenny's confidence in herself as a reader grew and she began to decipher more and more of the print around her. Alerted by me to mail carrying personal messages, Jenny began to attempt to read the messages mailed to her by the school or brought home by Donny.

Christmas season of that second year marked the first time ever that Jenny, Big Donny, and Timmy got dressed up and attended a Christmas concert at Donny's school in which he was performing with the rest of his class. This was also a first for Donny. He usually did not take part in such events, because no one at home had any idea they were occurring. All of this was made possible when Jenny dug the notice announcing the performance out of Donny's jeans pocket one night and read it through.

In addition, Jenny took a major personal step during

this second year that served to bring written text which was connected to her life on an intimate level into her home. After many years of vacillating about going to church, Jenny decided to join a Jehovah's Witness congregation. A friend of hers had described the church to her, and Jenny became interested after attending a few of the services.

Her family had always had Bibles in their homes, according to Jenny. Although this text was not accessible to Jenny or Big Donny, it was one of its teachings that allowed Jenny to choose to attend the Jehovah's Witnesses church, with the heavy time commitment required. Jenny explained this to me when I inquired about Big Donny's feelings about her going to church, which he himself did not want to attend:

> Well, he ain't got no choice with that. He don't have no say. That's the only thing that a woman can decide. That's the only thing you can have besides yourself. When you're married, you have to do what your husband tells you no matter what. 'Cause when you get married, you joinin' into one—somethin' like that. 'Cause God made woman before man. The man's the head of the household. But your husband cannot tell you what church to attend. Ever'body's got their own. She choose whatever religion she want. I'm talkin' in God's way.

I asked her if this was something she had just learned in church. No, she explained, it was in the Bible, and "We always had Bibles."

Jenny approved of the practice of the Jehovah's Witnesses of requiring potential members to study the church's teachings before joining.

> A lot of churches, you can go a month and they'll baptize you! But them [Jehovah's Witnesses], they want you to know and understand what you're gettin' yourself into before you get baptized. They don't try to lie to you and this 'n that. Like my sister Wanda went on down to the Holiness church, and I think they was goin' maybe three months and she got baptized. But yet, she [didn't know about it], 'cause I would ask more questions that I *already* know, and she didn't know 'em [the answers].

Once a week, two ladies from the church, one white and the other African American, would visit Jenny at home to study. Jenny wrote about Mary and Les in her journal in the Center, and her enthusiasm for this new learning shone through her text (typed version):

> When Mary and Les come to my house, we sit down at the table. We talk for a few minutes. Then one of them will say a prayer in Jesus Christ's name. You are supposed to pray through Jesus' name so that God can hear you. I think that is why you say Jesus' name when you pray. I will ask Mary on Friday. I have learned that God's name is Jehovah, and that woman is supposed to do what her husband tells her. If he tells her to do something that she knows is wrong, meaning if he says for her to smoke, well that would be against God because smoking is bad for you. God don't want you to do wrong, not even for your husband. God wants you to go by his rules. I

> feel if you have a heart then you know what God asks of us.

The study sessions with Mary and Les centered on written text. Jenny shared with me some of the pamphlets left by the two women explaining the church's position on such issues as the taboo against blood transfusions. In addition to these, Jenny worked with a text in which Bible passages are reprinted and study questions provided for the reader.

This mediation of print between Jenny and her religion carried over outside of her home, also, into the church services she attended once a week with Donny and Timmy. Jenny described what they did in church for me one day in her journal (typed version):

> The first hour, they talk about verses out of the Bible and stuff. Then the second hour is the *Watchtower.* You read and then they ask questions and you can raise your hand if you know it. Even Donny, he'll sometimes raise his hand. 'Cause there's one man that'll read the whole thing and you just follow along.

Jenny struggled through the reading at home with Mary and Les. She knew she was able to read only a small portion of the text on her own. But she continued to apply herself, often practicing in spare moments pieces of text she had gone over with her study partners earlier.

Jenny and Donny's home now looked different in terms of written language. Before, print had certainly been present in their house—on food items and circulars delivered by mail, on calendars and bills to pay, within the many children's books collected by Jenny and the old books collected by Big Donny. But because no one could or did use that print for any purpose, it did not exist for the people who lived in the house. Now, however, some print was visible to Jenny and her family. To the extent to which it was used for intentional, real-life purposes, written language now coded their world and was now available to them.

7

Who Reads and Writes in My World?

The discouraging outcome of one of my early interventions with Donny provides insight into his degree of success at learning to read and write. Soon after meeting Donny and Jenny and confirming Donny's delayed acquisition of critical concepts regarding print, I naively gave Jenny several specific suggestions regarding his home environment. I told her to provide materials with which Donny could experiment and practice emerging literacy skills. I suggested making paper and pencils, markers, crayons, and pens available to him.

These suggestions sprang from several sources of inspiration. First, all of the literature on emergent literacy in the home describes how young children will experiment with symbol making—drawing and writing—during the preschool years. Analysis of their products has detailed the developmental progression toward conventional uses of print by these children.[1]

As far back as 1966, Dolores Durkin's research into children who learn to read before experiencing formal instruction led her to describe these children as "paper and pencil" kids.[2] From an early age they were engaged in writing-type activities such as copying forms and letters, making lists, and writing their names and little messages. In more recent years, Denny Taylor has described the many ways in which the children in her family literacy study experimented with writing attempts.[3] All of the studies note the importance of making writing materials available to young children for their self-directed activity.

Second, the theory supporting the emergent literacy lens states that it is mainly through intentional, self-motivated activity that children begin to sort out for themselves a complex system such as reading and writing written language. For example, it is apparently through the use of such activities as inventive spelling that children begin to sort out the match between speech and print. Being able to do this gives them the freedom to explore the medium of print and test their hypotheses as to its nature. The result for the child is an increased understanding and control of print.

Although I was giving Donny the opportunity and encouragement to do this exploring in the Literacy Center, I felt that he needed to engage in it at home as well in order to make the frequency of these opportunities closer to that of those made available to his peers from literate, more mainstream homes. These suggestions were made, however, before I completely understood the significance of the nonliteracy in Donny's world. My grasp of this came slowly as I observed and documented, over time, both Donny's and Jenny's responses to instruction and their ways of negotiating their world. One critical moment in my dawning realization of the immensity of the situation occurred during the summer after our first year of working together.

Soon after my suggestion to Jenny, she had purchased paper, notebooks, and various markers and crayons at the Dollar Store down home. She set up a space in the bedroom upstairs for Donny to work with these and to store them. She explained that she could not keep them downstairs because, with all of the children running in and out during the day, they would soon be destroyed.[4] Donny reported proudly on his new "work desk" and appeared to be excited about the materials. I felt a certain smug satisfaction with my intervention and was impressed with Jenny's determination to follow my suggestions.

Six months later, I was visiting with Jenny over the kitchen table and needed a pencil to write something down. Jenny called to Donny to get "one of those pencils you had." Donny ran upstairs and came down with a fishing tackle box and showed me that he had put his pencil into the box along with some old rusty knives and fish hooks, among other things. My heart sank as he explained to me how he and Tommy used the pencils as fishing poles, tying string to them and pretending to fish in the backyard. Later, Jenny confirmed that she just could not get Donny to write at home as he did in the Center. The paper had been used for crafts, and the pencils and markers had either been lost or assumed other roles.

This episode helps to explain a consistent phenom enon running through the data on Donny's progression toward full literacy: his passive-aggressive resistance to reading and writing. I described in Chapter 4 Donny's impressive and steady development of concepts critical to literacy acquisition after he began at the Center. By the end of the first year, he was ready, in my opinion, to consolidate disparate skills into a move toward independent, conventional reading. By the middle of the second year of our association, he was technically a reader and a writer. The key to his continued development was time spent actually *doing* reading and writing. Yet this is exactly what he chose not to do.

Donny's resistance to becoming a reader/writer only became apparent to me around the time that I knew he could read and write the texts with which he was presented. This was during the summer following the first year. Looking back, however, I could see clear signs of this problem from the beginning. At the time I had interpreted the avoidance behavior as a reasonable reaction to being asked to do something that he did not understand and could not do.

Donny's initial indication that reading and writing were not attractive possibilities for him could be seen in his predilection for activities other than reading and writing. As I described in Chapter 4, when given the chance, Donny would choose to make things with the paper and materials available rather than use them as literacy tools. These moves on his part occurred with surprising swiftness. On one occasion, while I walked over to the bookshelf to retrieve another book to read to him, he moved quickly to the writing table. When I investigated, I discovered him making a pile of paper dots with the hole punch. His plan, he announced, was to glue them all on the paper. Throughout our two-year association, Donny proved to be incredibly quick and resourceful as he sought opportunities to subvert literacy events into crafts events.

The second type of behavior mentioned earlier was Donny's active avoidance of the print I made available to him. One of the earliest, and most graphic, examples of this occurred after we had worked together for about three months.

Donny had been listening to one of his favorite authors on tape. This particular author would read the text of a simple, predictable book several times through, often accompanied by a guitar emphasizing the beat and pattern to the language. Donny loved these "readings" and would often read/sing along with the tape, turning the pages as instructed. But when the time came for Donny to read the text himself, his first reaction was always to decline.

One day, after he had listened to a tape/text by this author, I asked him to read the text to me. I finger-pointed the words as I waited for him to begin. Turning his head away and covering his eyes, he exclaimed, "No, no! No words for me!"

It is hard to learn to read when you refuse to look at the words. I reasoned, however, that as he learned through many successful experiences that he *could* read, he would drop his reluctance. Yet this did not happen.

Documentations of reading and writing episodes during Donny's second year in the Literacy Center reveal similar patterns of behavior. When reading, Donny would only peripherally attend to the print, guessing his way through and supplying his own words. When I would bring him back to the print and make it clear that he was to read what was on the page, he would do so, demonstrating his ability.

The following episode illustrates Donny's typical way of avoiding the use of print as a primary source of information in his world. He had requested a certain book for me to read to him and was searching through the books on the book display table where he had last seen it.

V: "Did you find the one you wanted?"
D: "Yep; the one about outer space."
V: (Again, focusing him on the print, in this case splashed across the front of the book in bright red) "Do you know what the name of this book could be?"
D: "No."
V: "Could you guess?"
D: "*Comets.*"
V: "That's right. Why didn't you say that first?"
D: "I had to look at the pictures."

His avoidance of writing on his own was ingenious and tenacious. As he improved in his ability to encode language, his resistance to doing so increased. His tactics never included outright defiance but rather clever diversions and stallings to "run out the clock."

As a teacher, I continually sought to counter this behavior, which I experienced as a "holding back" by Donny. I searched for opportunities to make reading and writing personally meaningful for him, desirable, and enjoyable. I had already succeeded in making literacy possible, I believed, by bringing him conceptually to the point where the uses and functions of print in our society were demonstrated and by giving him many opportunities to join in these events while coming to understand the code aspect of print on several different levels. Ever elusive, though, was my ability to make Donny *want* to read and write.

As a researcher, I sought to understand this behavior, this holding back. I was drawn to B. M. Ferdman's guiding questions (see Appendix) regarding the mediation of cultural identity in the process of becoming literate. I rephrased the question from Donny's perspective, "Who reads and writes in my world?" The answer, for Donny, was, "No one important."

This issue was more complex than a simple lack of literate models in the home. The very core of Donny's identity was bound up with that of his parents. He loved his parents intensely and allied himself with them at all times. And as a male child, his identity was increasingly tied to his father, who had repeatedly announced his lack of desire to learn to read. Donny's growing male identity made Jenny's desire to learn to read less impressive for him.

His sensitive nature played a role here. Jenny's

candor about her inability to read was often quite painful for Donny, especially when she included Big Donny in her report of nonliteracy. At times, he would jump into the discussion with a deflection of, "Mom! You can read that *other* book all the way through!" At other times, he would attempt to create a sense of normalcy about the situation. One day Jenny explained to me that although Big Donny would not tell people that he was unable to read, "It don't bother me to tell people." At that point, Donny jumped in with, "It don't bother me too!"[5]

Donny's tales about the wonderful adventures he shared with his dad made exciting listening and reading. Many of his journal entries documented these exploits.

> The Cave Adventure
>
> We was driving down a road. And then we saw a cave. And my Dad stopped. My Dad didn't want to go in it. I got out of the truck. I went in it. My Dad followed me in it, too. We saw carvings on the wall. We looked at them. We touched them to see how old they are. If they are bumpy, they are really, really old. If they are not bumpy, people have carved over them. We came out of the cave and got in our truck. This is the end.

About a month following our first visit to the library, I asked Donny if he had been back. He said, yes, that his dad had taken him to the library twice while his mother was working. His dad had gotten his own library card, Donny reported. Intrigued, I asked Jenny later if this had actually happened.

Jenny explained that, no, Big Donny did not do much with the boys, despite their requests. Donny, in particular, wanted much more from his father, and Jenny was always asking Big Donny to take him along when he went fishing or camping with his brothers and friends. Only rarely would Big Donny agree to this. As the years of our association progressed, Donny's tales about his adventures with his dad and the many things his dad did became more frequent and fanciful.

Over time, as he matured, Donny's identity moved ever closer to his dad's, as Donny experienced him. Big Donny hunted, fished, and drove four-wheelers. Donny documented his own exploits hunting, fishing, and driving four-wheelers (Jenny: "It's a lie"). Big Donny whittled and carved with a knife. Donny informed me that he was spending his summer chopping wood off of a tree to carve with his knife. "It's easy!" he claimed. He said he was going to be an artist when he grew up like his dad and his uncles. (Jenny: "He's lucky if he can make a toothpick!")

Big Donny liked to draw to relax at home. Donny was drawing "army men" when I visited his house. "That's what I do when I stay home, huh, Ma?" he explained.

Big Donny liked to watch natural history movies and videos on television. Jenny explained to me that Donny liked them too and always watched along with his dad.

When Jenny told Big Donny that he ought to go back to school to learn to read, he put her off with the claim that he didn't have time and it didn't matter anyway. When Jenny reported to me that she could never get Donny to write at home, he agreed by shaking his head. "Don't have no time!" he said. I repeated back that he was a "busy man." "Yep! Playing!" was his response.

Big Donny did not read or write. Donny did not read or write except under duress, to which, as a child, he was subject. As a participating member of his culture as he experienced it, Donny saw himself as a "doer" and a "maker" and not as a reader or a writer. In his world, this was what people, adults, did. He was very "handy" and possessed a level of knowledge about roofing, cars, and machinery that often surpassed mine. All of his adult male relatives carved from wood and were self-reliant in the repair of cars, household appliances, and other machinery. This was Donny's world, and he liked it.

Interpreting the episode with which I began this chapter, I concluded that *my* cultural tools of literacy, when interjected into Donny's world, became *his* cultural tools. My pencils for writing became his fishing poles for fishing or pieces of wood for carving. My paper for writing became his material for the cutting, pasting, and forming of objects. And why not? For each of us, for all cultures, tools become tools only as they serve existing functions or needs. Donny perceived certain functions as culturally legitimate; he adapted the materials around him to serve these functions. As Donny perceived his culture and his role in it, he did not see reading and writing as legitimate.

Given this view of himself as a cultural being, Donny

was missing the crucial element of intentionality from his literacy development. He could acquire the concepts about written language he had missed earlier when they were purposefully and directly presented to him in the Literacy Center. Outside of artificial instructional settings, however, reading and writing was, for the most part, irrelevant. As much as Jenny would exhort him to apply himself to learn to read and write so that he could do what his parents could not, Donny made a choice and took a stance. He chose to stand with his parents and, especially, with his dad. Literacy for Donny, as for his parents, was not what one did if given the choice.

8

Exclusion and Access

This close account of Jenny and Donny as literacy learners, contextualized by their sociocultural experiences and roles, began with the question, "What does the world look like through the eyes of a nonliterate, gendered, urban Appalachian?" A further question is, "Does the answer to this help to explain their difficulties learning to read and write?" I believe it does.

The image of an *outsider* best captures my sense of this story. Jenny and her family experience the urban literate world as foreigners—as outsiders to a world that does not recognize them or include them. This world, to Jenny, in particular, is impermeable and resistant to her attempts to enter. Its members do not live as she does or talk as she does. Its ways of doing business, of conducting interpersonal relationships and communications, is confusing and alien. Not only are the rules different, but this world employs an unreadable written code for conducting much of this business. Jenny cannot function effectively in this world. She cannot make herself heard, nor can she accomplish her personal goal of literacy for herself and her child.

Jenny and her family's outsider status results from a complex interplay of factors emanating from both their own cultural identity and that assigned to them from the literate mainstream. Jenny, and many of those identified as urban Appalachian, feel truly displaced in the city and wish to live "down home" again. In a very real sense, they maintain their outsider status through their own efforts to sustain their country ties while considering their urban lives only temporary, even across generations of city dwellers.

Jenny, however, wanted something from the city, specifically from the city schools. She wanted literacy, for herself and for her children. She did not want to "become" middle class. She did not want to change herself, her way of life, her cultural "ways of being," or her language. She only wanted to learn to read and write for her own needs and desires. This goal, however, proved elusive, given the cultural and societal walls standing between her and the literacy controlled by the mainstream schools.

Jenny's desire for literacy, both for herself and for her child, was impeded by a wall of exclusion erected by a society and an educational system that willfully failed to *see* her and Donny, and thus to consider and include them.

Exclude includes in its meaning all of the following: disapprove, reject, prohibit, bar, banish, and prevent.

Jenny and Donny were recipients of all of these actions at the hands of the educational establishment. Donny and Jenny as learners, each in his or her own time, and Jenny as a mother stood outside of a solid wall of indifference and cultural elitism and ignorance. An account of Jenny's frustration with the school's non-response to her concern about Donny's failure to learn vividly captures the essence of this wall.

Banging on the School Door

According to Jenny, she was first spurred to action when she arrived with Donny for the first day of school following his first-grade year. She understood that he had failed and fully expected to take him to one of the first-grade classrooms. Instead, when she arrived at the door of his assigned room, she saw that it was the second-grade classroom. Her first thought was that a mistake had been made. But when she checked with the office, she was informed that, no, this was the right assignment.

Flabbergasted, she protested to the front office personnel, but to no avail. Demanding to speak with the principal, she was eventually told by the secretary that the decision "had been made" for Donny to continue in second grade until the end of the first quarter, at which time "they" would decide if he should be put back into first grade. It was at this point that she sought out the Literacy Center.

Jenny could not believe that the people at the school did not see that Donny did not know what he needed to know to succeed in second grade. They were just "jackasses," she concluded, for putting him in a no-win situation. "He don't know *any* of them words!" She had told his teacher that if they didn't put him back (in first grade), "I was goin' to raise hell with 'em . . . and I'd go to the Board of Education."

At the end of the first quarter, no one suggested moving Donny back to first grade, although Jenny continued to protest to the office and to his teacher.

As the year drew to a close, Jenny insisted on a meeting with Ms. Black to discuss retaining Donny in second grade. When Jenny asked Ms. Black when they could meet, though, "She said she was going to go ahead and fail him. She said he wasn't mature enough."

By the start of the following school year, both Jenny and I fully expected Donny to repeat second grade which, as explained in Chapter 4, I saw as requisite to his "catching up" to the curriculum. Yet the same thing happened again: Jenny called me at home to report Donny's placement into third grade. Her inherent refusal to accept nonsense came through when we later met in person to discuss the situation:

> Somebody needs to investigate that school! 'Cause when I went in the office that day, I told that lady . . . 'cause I couldn't find his name on that second grade (list) . . . 'cause of he failed. And I went in there an' I was tellin' her. She said, "No, no kids failed last year." An' I said, "Huh?" She said, "No." An' I couldn't say nothin' 'cause I couldn't even

> breathe [she was suffering from pneumonia and asthma at the time]. 'Cause I know *some* kids failed! Like him (indicating Donny). An' she said, "No kids failed last year." An' I thought, "That's stupid!"

Jenny had asked to see the principal but was told that he was out of his office, supervising on the playground. When she asked when he would be back, she was told that a good time to catch him would be between 1:00 and 1:30. She said she would be there. I had offered to accompany her to a meeting with the principal, so she called me to give me this time. I arranged to pick her up at home as she had no transportation for this time of day.

Later the same morning, I decided to call the school to make sure that the principal would be in. The secretary took my call and reported that no appointment was noted between Jenny and the principal. In fact, she went on, the principal already had a 1:00 appointment.

"This is Dr. Victoria Purcell-Gates," I informed her, "Director of the University Literacy Center." I told her that I had been working with Donny Browning and that I wished to attend a meeting between Mrs. Browning and the principal to express my belief that Donny should repeat second grade.

The secretary recalled that his mother had been in the office several times "on the issue of retention." She thought it had "been handled." She would call me back after she spoke with the principal about an appointment time.

We never met with the principal. According to his secretary, he declared, when informed of my interest, "If she wants him held back, then we'll do it. No problem."

Jenny was astonished. She had "been on them so long and now all of a sudden. . . ." Ascribing an inflated degree of control to me, she concluded, "He's probably scared of gettin' his ass kicked!"

She exploded, though, when I told her that the secretary was waiting for her to call and tell her that she wanted Donny moved back before she began the paperwork. "The whole durn *school* knows I want him held back!" she exclaimed.

Jenny, as a concerned mother, had not merely been ignored. Rather, my sense was that, as a concerned mother, she had been invisible to the secretary, the principal, the teacher—the school bureaucracy. As noted in Chapter 2, urban Appalachians are widely viewed by school personnel as unfit parents who care little about education. Therefore Jenny, as a concerned mother, did not exist. Her continual presence in the school office was experienced only as a mildly irritating anomaly. Her complaint that Donny had not learned anything in first grade and thus could not possibly succeed in second was never heard, considered, or countered. Certainly Donny's promotions through the grades were not the result of carefully thought out decisions. The principal's rapid capitulation to my over-the-phone request that Donny be retained was proof of this.

Jenny's treatment as a nonperson was instantiated

on a daily basis as Donny's teachers sent homework and office personnel sent written notices home to parents who, as they had "plainly told" them, could not read.

Jenny struggled with her inability to help Donny with his homework. Time and again, she told his respective teachers that Donny did not complete his homework because she could not read well enough to help him and Donny could not do it on his own. Time and again, Donny arrived home with mimeographed sheets of homework that were useless to him. Time and again, notations were made for school records and on report cards explaining failing grades that "Donny needs to *try;* Donny does not complete homework." And in ignoring Jenny's concern as well as her son's predicament, teachers and school administrators collected more "evidence" that Appalachian parents are irresponsible and uncaring about their children's education.

Jenny's anger over this situation simmered. Referring to his teacher and the work she had sent home one day, she declared, "She *knows* I can't read, but she still sends this stuff home! I can't make him do it; he's supposed to do it himself, but he *can't.*" Jenny never understood how the school could refuse to teach Donny at a level at which he could learn (by retaining him) and at the same time expect him and his parents to perform at a level they could not.

The failure of the school to see and/or hear her led to a potentially disastrous event toward the end of Donny's first year at the Literacy Center. One day,

Jenny appeared with Donny for a session. As was her custom, she handed me some papers from the school for me to read to her before I began to work with Donny.

To my consternation, one of the papers announced Donny's suspension from school. It was a copy of a form report with his name, his teacher's name, his grade, room number, and the date filled in the blanks. His teacher had filled in: "In the class room, he was fighting and would not stop." After *Corrective Measures,* she had written: "Tried reasoning, didn't work, would not stop." After *Action,* office personnel had written, "3 day removal." I explained to Jenny that this meant that he had been suspended.

"He said he couldn't go back to school until Saturday, and I couldn't read it so I didn't know what it meant," she added.

Together we worked out that the three-day suspension would end on the following Tuesday due to a Monday holiday. Going through the remaining papers, I discovered a form letter to the parents which announced that Jenny must attend a scheduled "hearing" before Donny would be allowed back in school. Without me as a reader and a translator, Jenny would never have known about the suspension or the required conference because both were announced through print, even though all of the office personnel and the teacher had been repeatedly informed that neither Jenny nor Big Donny could read.

Jenny, reflecting the weight Appalachians place on personal relationships, sought to make the school bureaucracy hear her or see her as a legitimate parent with real concerns about her child's education. She told them *in person* about the needs she and Donny had. She was never acknowledged.

The school personnel, working within a literate middle-class bureaucratic system, could not understand that there might be another world view present that could account for behaviors and expectations. Further, from this middle-class perspective, Jenny and Donny, as urban Appalachians, were seen as simple instances of an amorphous group, about which a multitude of negative stereotypes were held. Although urban Appalachians were seen as individuals with educational needs, these were needs that were beyond the school. Members of this "invisible minority" were seen as failures from the beginning, including Donny at age seven, failures that, as the educational hierarchy perceived it, continue to plague urban schools and make them look bad.

A Wall of Discourse

Language often served as the mode of exclusion for Jenny and Donny. Language is a highly visible marker of culture, and therefore this effect is not surprising. Because reading and writing are language processes, however, the utilization of language as an exclusionary force made learning to read and write extremely difficult, if not impossible, for Jenny and Donny. This exclusion occurred on the level of both oral dialect and written style.

Exclusionary Oral Dialect Attitudes

The teacher who declared, "I *knew* she [Jenny] was ignorant as soon as she opened her mouth!" harshly revealed how oral dialects and our responses to them are used to exclude. The Appalachian dialect has been used in movies, television shows, and books to mark its users as ignorant, lazy, incestuous, violent, and generally worthless. The American public has developed a near conditioned response to it. This was certainly true in the urban context in which Jenny and Donny found themselves.

In one account after another, urban Appalachians have recalled the ridicule and punishment they faced in city schools whenever they spoke or read aloud. A young woman's story of her despair over the city school's use of her language to discount her sounds hauntingly similar to Jenny's:

> Mother and Daddy moved up to Ohio when I was a junior [in high school]. I just couldn't deal with it. I went to school, but I just couldn't fit in. At home [Kentucky], I was good in school, even a year ahead for my age. When I got up there, they did everything different. Sometimes I couldn't understand what the teacher said; they talked so fast and said words different. The worst part was the way they made fun of me for my accent. One teacher [made] me read out loud to the class to help me with my reading. I could read, I just couldn't say the words right. Every time I said a word wrong she would make me say it over and over. I tried. I really tried. I just couldn't. I

> would leave crying almost every day. She called me ignorant in front of everybody. She said I was illiterate and that I would never learn, that I was hopeless. I'll never forget it. Not ever. . . . They [Mother and Daddy] let me come back [to Kentucky]. They knew I wouldn't stay in that school another year. I still hate to go out of the mountains. There are words I won't say 'cause I don't say them right. Like *f-r-u-s-t-r-a-t-e-d.* I wouldn't ever try to say that word.[1]

Jenny blamed her "countrified words" for her inability to learn to read, shouldering the blame placed upon her by her teachers. It had never occurred to her that her language was legitimate enough to be written and read. To Jenny and to members of the mainstream society, both, her dialect marked her as unable and unwilling to learn. It was used as a wall to exclude her from access to an effective education.

Exclusionary Written Language Style

As impenetrable as the wall of cultural and linguistic elitism for Jenny was the barrier erected by the style of written text, particularly bureaucratic text. Jenny's oral dialect was an integral part of her and her home culture, and society's reaction to it was governed by political and social factors. Her inexperience with written style, in contrast, was the direct result of her nonliteracy. And in an ironic twist, the characteristics of written style made her acquisition of literacy all the more difficult.

Literacy opens up a world of language to readers not available in a purely oral culture.[2] Written language employs more varied vocabulary and a level of vocabulary that can be described as "literary" or "written." Words like *employ, participate,* and *acquisition* are more likely to appear in print than in one's conversation, where they would likely be replaced by *use, join in,* and *learn* or *get,* as we saw in Chapter 3. As one learns, or "acquires," vocabulary items after encountering them in print, it is not unusual for these items to appear in one's oral language, depending on the appropriateness of the social situation. The more literate family members are, and the more they read, the greater will be the infusion of literary vocabulary in their speech.

The reverse is also true. Although both of Jenny's parents had been able to read, neither had graduated from high school and, as far as she could remember, they only read minimally from brochures and a few magazines. Jenny's exposure to the varied and literary vocabulary associated with written text was almost nil. She did not hear it in the oral speech of her family members as a child or learn it through her own reading.

Another distinguishing feature of written language is its structure. Written language units are much more "packed"; that is, they contain more words per unit than comparable spoken units. Further, the units are often ordered in ways not found in spoken language. Very seldom will one find the following ordering of clauses and phrases in the language of a speaker:

> A quarter of a mile away lay a bounded bay with a beach bordered by forest.[3]

This sentence, taken from a children's book, embodies the inversions and orderings typical of written text.

The more formal the written language becomes, the more features "typical" of written language appear.[4] Thus, as many readers are painfully aware, bureaucratic and academic writing is the most "written" of written text. By virtue of this, it is the most impenetrable to outsiders, those not members of the bureaucracy or academic field.

As Jenny's ability to read her own language and that of my written responses and notes grew, her difficulty with the features of written text became more apparent. This difficulty significantly hindered her church-related reading, one of the first functional literacy events to enter her home. Sharing with me the text she had read with Mary and Les, one day, Jenny pointed out the word *desire* in the sentence *What desire do people normally have?* She told me that she had not known what that word was until Mary pronounced it and explained that it meant *wish*. The word *wish* was written over the word *desire*, and Jenny read the sentence substituting *wish* for *desire*.

Reflecting on the difficulty she had reading the church material, Jenny commented, "I'll be aggravatin' myself real bad; 'cause like them words I don't know? Like the verses in the Bible. I try to read them, try to understand, and I can't get enough of it to make a thought. Like the words I don't know, they're the main ones you gotta know to know what the sentence says!"

The written school "communications" sent to her were typically bureaucratic in style. This was text she needed to read, both to gain access to the culture of the school and to obtain help for her son. Also, as with the church-related readings, this text represented much of the functional reading in her life, and she needed to read it in order to integrate the reading strategies she was learning in the Center to advance her level of literacy. Even when this text was read to her, however, she found it virtually impossible to understand.

Probably the incident that most captures the impenetrable nature of written style for Jenny involves a questionnaire that she received toward the end of the first year of our association. As was her custom, Jenny brought papers for me to read to one of Donny's sessions. These papers included an official-looking questionnaire issued by the school district and given to the children to take home.

The following excerpts vividly illustrate instances of both Jenny's difficulties with written style and the cultural distance between Jenny and the public school establishment. Repeatedly, Jenny would answer the questions on a purely personal level, requiring my translation to understand the intent of the questionnaire as well as the vocabulary. Her humor and honesty come through in many of her responses. I began by reading the cover page for the questionnaire, explaining it and providing directions. Note the language of the text:

V (reading): Dear Parents/Guardians:

For many years, parents and guardians of ——— Public School children have participated in our annual parent survey. This survey gives you the opportunity to let us know how you feel about your child's schooling. It's like our report card prepared by you. Within our means, we will correct any deficiencies which are expressed by parents and thus better serve our pupils. Your attitudes and judgments will help us determine the extent to which the goals we have set for our schools are being met. When the surveys are returned the results will be tabulated then reported to the principal as soon as possible. Your principal will let you know when the results are available. . . . Your honest and frank answers to these questions will not reflect on your child in any way since you will not be identified. Do not sign your name. Simply fill out the survey now and ask your child to return it to school no later than Friday of this week. Please do not bend, fold, or tear the survey since it will be scored by machine. Please mark your survey with a pencil. Thank you for taking your time to participate in the survey.

J: O.K. So what is it?

V: It's a questionnaire to see how you feel about things about the school. And you're not supposed to sign your name so it won't affect your child if you say bad things about it.

J: Well, how do they know who did it then?

V: They don't care who did it. They just want to collect as many as they can.
J: Oh, I see.

After directing Jenny where to fill in Donny's grade, sex, race, and school, I asked her to read the questions, which she did with my help on certain, usually literary-type, words. I have italicized the words that I helped her with.

V: O.K., Number one. . .
J: "Does your child attend an *alternative program?*" What does that mean?
V: There's different alternative schools like a Montessori school and things like that, but I think this is a regular neighborhood school.
J: Probably
V: The other schools are public but you have to ask to go there.
J: No, it's not. So what do I put there?
V: You have a choice of 'Y,' 'N,' or 'U' for 'yes,' 'no,' or 'undecided.'
J: So I put an 'N,' huh?
V: Yeah.
J: "Does your child's school teach what you think should be taught?"
V: Right.
J: I don't know. (pause) Heck, I don't know.
V: Is there anything that you think should be taught that doesn't get taught?
J: I don't know what all they supposed to teach! I don't know all that. That's why I'm trying to go back myself.
V: O.K. Then maybe a 'U' would be best there for 'undecided.'

J: "Are you *satisfied* with the *quality* of teaching at your child's school?" I didn't even understand what I just read! "Are you satisfied with the quality. . ." What's that word mean?

V: How good it is.

J: No. So what do I mark it, 'N'?

V: Right.

J: No, 'cause she hasn't passed Danny (back). I marked it right.

[. . .]

J: "Do you feel there is good *discipline* at your child's school?" "Discipline". . . mean makin' 'em behave?

V: Uh huh.

J: The 'N'! 'Cause twice down there already he's been knocked down on the playground. There's supposed to be people out there watchin' them so they don't do that.

"Do you feel your child is safe at school?" Uh hum, yeah, I guess he is. So what do I mark. Oh, a 'Y.' Why don't they just put a 'yes' or 'no'?

V: 'Cause it wouldn't fit in there.

I left her to work on the questionnaire alone while I saw to Donny. When I returned:

J: "Do you believe the staff at your child's school supports *interracial understanding*?" Now, what's that mean?

V: Staff is people who work there, including the secretaries and teachers. So, 'do they support interracial understanding' means do they help children between the different races, like black and white, get along.

J: The lady in the office does. Donny's teacher does. As far as the rest of them goes, I don't know.

V: I think you should put 'yes' then because as far as you know they do.
[. . .]

J: "Do you think your child's school does a good job teaching her/him to think *critically*?" What's 'critically' mean?

V: To think critically means, do you think they are doing a good job teaching them to think about what they learn and being able to decide for themselves what's right or wrong, true or not true. Just being able to think more for themselves. Or do you think they just teach stuff that they think everybody ought to know and not to think about it.

J: (Pause) If I had to sit in a classroom [at Donny's school] all day, I'd know that!

V: Yeah, so put a 'U.'
[. . .]

J: "Does your child's report card give you the kind of information you want?" No; he always gets F's and D's! (laughs) But I don't think that's what that means. What's that mean?

V: It means like is there other stuff you'd like to know about how he's doing in school that they don't even have on the report card.

J: I don't even know what's on the report card! I just know he gets F's and D's. I can't read all that stuff.

V: Why don't you put 'U' for that then.
[. . .]

J: "Have you *received* any information about your school's local advisory committee?" I don't know what that is.

V: So put a 'U.' Maybe you got it and just didn't read it.

J: Probably.

[. . .]

J: "Do you believe your child's teachers take a *personal interest* in him/her?" Does that mean do I think she pays more attention to one kid than another?

V: No, it means does she pay attention to him. Is she interested in Donny as Donny?

J: Well, she knows he's got problems. She stands up in front of the class and tells them what to do but as far as comin' to each child, I don't think so.

V: O.K., then put 'N.'

[. . .]

J: "Do you understand your child's *achievement* test score reports?"

V: Remember the test scores that you brought in at the beginning of the year for me? When those came home, did you understand them?

J: No, I couldn't read them. "Has the school *adequately* . . ." I don't know what them words are.

V: 'Adequately' means enough. If you're thirsty and I gave you a glass of water, I could ask you, "Was that adequate?" Enough not to make you thirsty? If not, you would say it was "inadequate."

J: Oh, why do they use such words?

[. . .]

V: You must be getting tired.

J: Oh, I've *been* tired!

V: So let me read these to you. "Do you feel your child is safe in the school's immediate neighborhood?"

J: No, I don't.

V: "Are you aware of opportunities to volunteer at your child's school?"

J: Mean 'help out'? No. They might, but I can't read it. [. . .]

V: "Do you feel that the drug/alcohol program at your child's school is effective?"

J: I don't even know if they got one.

V: "Do you know what is expected of your child in his/her classes at school?"

J: No.

V: "Do you monitor your child's homework assignments regularly?"

J: What does that mean?

V: Do you check his assignments everyday.

J: No, 'cause I think he's supposed to write spelling words and sentences on different days, but I can't help him if I can't read it. So what would you put?

V: Well, it seems like you always look at it but sometimes you just can't help him with it. So it does seem that you check on it so I would put 'yes.'

"Are you aware of the discipline plan at your child's school?"

J: What they're allowed to do and what they ain't allowed to do? I don't know.

V: "Have you served as a volunteer in your child's school this past school year?"

J: I never knew they wanted one.

Jenny "never knew" most things concerning participation within the educational mainstream culture that held the key to literacy for her and her children. Her access to this information was blocked in many cases, as the one above, by her lack of experience with and knowledge of the written language that encoded this information.

Jenny was not the only one who never knew, however. Donny's teachers, and I suspect Jenny's before him, never knew what to do for him. Seeing only through middle-class lenses, and following the strict scope and sequence of a preplanned beginning literacy curriculum, they could not account for his lack of progress with anything except judgments about his failure to try, to "stay on task," and to do his homework. In my interviews with teachers and staff, I encountered no real understanding of the significant ways in which the school curriculum was failing to meet Donny's cognitive needs. Nor did I detect any genuine attempt to gain insight in ways not suggested by "traditional" (mainstream) means of evaluation and assessment.

The irrelevancy of the curriculum to Donny's chances of learning to read and write—so obvious to me—was incomprehensible to teachers unused to looking outside of their assigned curriculums for insights into learning and development. With a dearth of knowledge about oral/written language differences and the many concepts concerning written language and its use learned by children merely by participating in literate homes, these teachers were in no position to appreciate the repercussions of growing up in a home where neither parent read or wrote for any reason.

Their only response in the face of Donny's failure to "catch on" (when finally forced to respond by me, representing Jenny) was to provide him with more intensive instruction in the same irrelevant curriculum for one year—and then to ignore him as the curriculum moved forward without him. Jenny recognized this immediately for exactly what it was—the same as experienced by her and Big Donny: ". . . they're just gonna pass him on. That don't do no good; I know!"

Thus access to literacy was blocked for Jenny and Donny by a confluence of factors that cast them in the role of outsiders. Instruction was controlled by a mainstream culture that erected a solid wall of cultural difference, cultural stereotype, cultural and linguistic elitism, and pedagogical ignorance and obtuseness. This wall was reinforced by Jenny and her family's indifference to "joining the mainstream" on the other side, and their own nonliteracy and inexperience with literate style.

When I first met them, neither Jenny nor Donny could read or write beyond their names. Jenny had experienced seven years of public school instruction and four of adult school. Donny had experienced one year of public school instruction, preceded by one year of Head Start. Their near total nonliteracy was a testament to the strength and effectiveness of the wall.

Breaching the Wall: Making Connections

To begin to develop as readers and writers, Donny and Jenny needed to breach this wall that stood between them and the literate world. They needed to see and experience the connectedness of literacy and life. They needed to bring print into *their* world; then, and only then, could they commence with learning to read and write the written code that had proved so elusive beforc from the outside. They did this, with my help, at the Literacy Center.

In an ironic, intuitive way, Jenny had pinpointed the source of her difficulty early on. Her words did act as a wall between her and functional literacy, because her own words were never acknowledged and affirmed, never allowed. When she tried to match her own phonological system to the one taught in the schools' phonics lessons, she failed. Not because she could not "hear" the system at the phonemic base, but because her system was different. It is true, however, that everyone's dialect varies from the phonological system inherent in phonics programs. Jenny needed to see that her words did map onto standard orthography just as others' do; she needed teachers to show her how that happened.

Jenny needed to read real text in order to learn to read. The texts given her to read earlier were not "real" to her. Not only could she not relate to them on a content level, she was so stuck at the "word" level that she was effectively paralyzed. She continued year after year trying to memorize words, trying to memorize rules, trying to memorize terms such as *adverb* and *pronoun*. Not one of these words, rules, or linguistic terms was hers, related to her in any way, and thus she could not succeed.

Donny needed instruction that could bring print into his world for the first time. Further, he needed instruction to point out to him the real-life uses of written language and the ways in which this language could encode his world. As was true for Jenny, his development as a reader and a writer depended on literacy, heretofore rooted in the experience, culture, and language of the literate mainstream barricaded behind the wall, crossing into his world in ways that made sense to him.

Jenny and Donny will continue to develop as readers and writers to the extent to which they build upon their beginnings and incorporate in increasing degrees meaningful, functional uses of print into their lives. As this occurs, *if* it occurs, they will shape the types of literacy they encounter to fit their world as well as be shaped in ongoing ways by their participation in a literate world.

9

The Complexities of Culture, Language, Literacy, and Cognition

Case studies allow us to look closely at a situation and seek to identify patterns of relationships between factors deemed important for the working of a particular phenomenon. The case of Jenny and Donny helps us look at the phenomenon of low literacy achievement of peoples from poor, minority, low-literate communities. By employing a sociocultural lens that allows us to see them as cultural beings whose identities and perceptions reflect the nested cultural contexts of ethnic heritage, education/literacy level, gender, and socioeconomic status, we gain insights into the ways they perceive the literate world and the world of school.

Throughout the history of literacy development worldwide, social class differences have consistently predicted literacy skill achievement.[1] If you are a child born into a family that is not middle class and educated, your chances of achieving a literacy level equal to that of another child born into such a family are low. In a country such as the United States, with its history of proclaimed egalitarianism and commitment to equal access to education and opportunity, this fact is galling and troublesome.

This portrait of Jenny's and Donny's experiences with learning to read and write spotlights a vastly underresearched population: poor whites. Most people in the United States are not used to thinking about whites as minorities or as the objects of prejudice and injustice. Undoubtedly, poor whites have not had to fight against discrimination based on skin color. This has made life, in many ways, infinitely easier for them, and one cannot assume that their perceptions of themselves and of others are the same as they are for African Americans, Latinos, Asian Americans, or Native Americans (nor can one say that life looks the same for members of different minorities of color).[2] It is equally true, however, that the literacy attainment of poor whites is significantly below that of middle-class whites, reflecting the socioeconomic status that they share with the many minorities of color.

Why social class difference in literacy achievement persists despite our continued efforts and vast amounts of money directed at "solving" the problem is a question plaguing politicians, sociologists, psychologists, anthropologists, religious leaders, educational leaders, practitioners, and theorists. The fact that it does persist bodes ill for the economic and social future of the United States. As global competition in a highly technological world continues to increase at an alarming rate, the crucial gap between the abilities of low-literate people and those of people of the educational elite is highlighted.

A number of theories exist to explain this problem, ranging from John Ogbu's theory of resistance among caste minorities to Paolo Freire's "pedagogy of the oppressed."[3] All of these theories aid us in understanding various aspects of Jenny and Donny's case, but their story also contributes insights of its own. Jenny and Donny's journeys and destinations as literacy learners in the context of U.S. city schools reveal a complex pattern of synergistic relationships among social, cultural, and cognitive/linguistic factors that explain the experience of this mother and son as outsiders to literacy.[4]

Cognition and the Culture of Literacy

The concept of the *foreigner,* or the *outsider,* captures in important ways the experience of many learners who have difficulty learning to read and write. Not only do they struggle to gain control over a strange code, but they also experience the world encoded by print as unfamiliar and unpredictable.[5] These learners are in a real sense *immigrants* to the literate world, with as much to learn about the culture of literacy as about the language of print. Because of the nature of their relationship, moreover, the culture of literacy and the language that encodes it must be learned and experienced as a whole, as one. In other words, unless one acquires literate behaviors, using print and participating with literate others, one cannot go beyond a simple, often incomplete, mastery of the code.

The work of the sociolinguist James Gee (1989) illuminates these findings. Gee claims that literacy is more than just reading and writing. Literacy is part of a larger "Discourse," which is a "way of being," a sociocultural "identity kit"—or, I believe, a series of nested cultural contexts. Thus Jenny and Donny's nonliteracy, which so influenced the way they perceived and processed information, was part of their Discourse. Gee believes that Discourses are not mastered by overt instruction that deals with the superficial aspects of grammar, style, and mechanics. Rather, one learns a Discourse by being enculturated into its social practices through scaffolding and social interaction with people who have already mastered the Discourse. In reflecting on Jenny's and Donny's journeys toward literacy, we may consider their experiences in the Literacy Center as providing the needed scaffolding and social interaction with literate others.

Children born into a rich and varied literate world, in the sense that important others in their lives use print often for many reasons, find learning to read and write in school relatively easy. They understand reading and writing as something one does just to live. It is a process over which they expect to gain control as soon as possible, like walking or driving. They already know, or acquire implicitly as they develop, the varying registers of written language with the accompanying "ways of meaning" and "ways of saying," the vocabulary, the syntax, the intentionality. This makes learning the "new" so much easier. At the beginning of formal schooling, these children need to focus simply on the ways in which print encodes a familiar language, about which they already know quite a bit. As this knowledge becomes automatic, they develop as users of print, learning new concepts and accompanying language as they read and write to learn and to communicate at increasingly more complex levels.

Children born into cultures that are low literate and/or restricted in their scope of literacy find themselves in an immigrant state. Learning to read and write is not as "natural" for them. The process requires much more attention, effort, and time. Their social and cultural lives do not support this effort but rather exist separately and often compete with it. From the beginning they are challenged to learn a code that some of them (like Donny) may not even have realized existed before. Others, from literate but less educated families, find that over time, the language and purposes for print encountered through formal education are foreign. The vocabulary is too hard and removed from their daily lives; the convoluted syntax of exposition and complex fiction is unfathomable. Without a great deal of support, motivation, and effort, their level of literacy skill attainment is bound to be low compared with that of their peers who are natives of the more educated literate world.

The profound correlation between social class and literacy level includes, then, the implication of social class in having difficulty in learning to read and write. Children from poor, minority homes have, overall, lower levels of literacy skill, and different ways of incorporating literacy into their lives as compared with their middle-class peers. Lower-class, minority homes will thus be, overall, differently literate, as communities, from middle-class ones. Children and adults in these low-income, minority, differently literate communities will experience greater difficulty learning to read and write in schools designed for children from middle-class literate homes.

Emergent Literacy

In many ways the case study of Jenny and Donny helps to confirm the major theoretical tenets of the field of emergent literacy. Above all, this account confirms the role of print in children's everyday lives in their ability to build conceptual understandings about reading and writing. It does this by showing us the effects of a virtual absence of print on children's ability to "take from" instruction.

This case study also contributes to emergent literacy theory by questioning the notion of a "print-rich" society. Jenny and Donny's experiences show us that print is present to an individual only to the extent that it is used by members of one's sociocultural group. In this sense, print does not exist independent of experience. The presence of print in Jenny and Donny's home did not mean that it was present for them in the same way that print is present for many of the families described in emergent literacy research.

Emergent literacy theory must begin to account for the variations of early literacy learning. We cannot continue to assert that all children in the United States learn many important concepts about written language before they begin school. Clearly Donny and Timmy did not, and several recent studies of the written language knowledge held by entering kindergartners, measured from an emergent literacy perspective, confirm that other young children vary in the degree to which they have learned about written language in their homes and communities.[6]

Emergent literacy research has allowed us to understand better the ways in which young children, in their daily lives at home and in community, build conceptual understandings about written language as they observe and participate in its use. Now we need to pay more attention to the "as they observe and participate in its use" aspect of this assertion. Emergent literacy theory must expand to include and explain more cases, and we can do this by exploring the factor of literacy function or use within children's lives.

The concept of *literacy use* is a valuable one in structuring the ways in which we portray, and think about, the knowledges about print that young children bring to school with them from their home cultures. Conceptualizing literacy as cultural behavior facilitates our ability to recognize the different ways in which print is and is not used by families. Going further and recognizing the ways in which literacy knowledge acquired by young children relates to these variants of print use will allow us to think about curriculum in ways that are individually responsive to children and that facilitate literacy development for all.

One caveat is particularly important here. Conceptualizing literacy as cultural practice denies any notion of deficit. A cultural perspective on behavior implies the study of *difference* rather than deficit. Jenny and Donny were not any more deficient than you or I would be in a culture other than our own. They simply did not possess the cultural knowledge needed to participate in a literate society or to learn from a literacy curriculum that presupposed such knowledge.

Although the absence of this cultural knowledge of print did not constitute a deficit on their part, it was important to recognize and acknowledge it as a crucial difference so that their failure to learn could be accounted for. This explanation led to the conscious effort to make written language functional *for them*. Once literacy began to function and mediate their culturally relevant social activities, they could begin to acquire skill in it.

Culture, Status, and School Success

Examining issues of low literacy achievement through a sociocultural lens implies that we also recognize the cultural view of reality held by those in control of education, teaching, and, ultimately, the children and their futures. Judgments of deficiency, dysfunction, and irresponsibility are all culturally relative stances. They are made by educators who cannot, or will not, step out of their ethnocentric world to attempt to see their students from another perspective. When one is a participating member of the sociocultural group in power, this may be an acceptable response to the failure of the schools. It is not a moral one, though, or an effective one, and serves only to perpetuate the situation.

Learners from low-caste minority communities experience difficulty attaining equal access to educational opportunities for a variety of complex social and political reasons. Particularly relevant to this discussion are the preconceived stereotypes of minority cultures held by mainstream members of society. These stereotypes interact in pernicious ways with minority learners' attempts to gain access to literacy and the literate world.

Donny and Jenny's case illustrated this well in part because the stereotypes held of Appalachians are still so prevalent in our society. The Appalachians are a low-status, minority group of whom those in the mainstream are less conscious, and hence in some respects less sensitive to, than groups such as African Americans, Latinos, and Native Americans. Partly, I suspect, this lack of awareness is due to the fact that Appalachians are overwhelmingly white and of European descent[7] and thus blend into the white mainstream whenever the problems and issues of ethnic minorities, or "people of color," are raised. Additionally, and perhaps more significantly, Appalachians themselves and urban Appalachians, in particular, have not formed political action groups intended to raise public consciousness about their culture and needs as members of an identified minority.[8]

The stereotyping of peoples from low-status groups occurs more openly for urban Appalachians today than for other ethnic minorities of whom society is slightly more conscious. We can still regularly hear references to "hillbillies" and their lack of drive, denigration of education, slovenliness, and poor parenting skills while public references to "niggers" or "drunken Injuns" are no longer openly socially acceptable.[9] Donny and Jenny's case allows us to see more clearly the effect of minority stereotyping on access to educational opportunity, an effect that is similar for all low-status minorities. This case study makes the effect of negative stereotyping—which is increasingly becoming "invisible," as it affects minorities of color—"visible."

Stereotyping is the result of a profound lack of knowledge about a particular group. The kinds of stereotypes held of minority, low-status groups by the mainstream and those whose business is education are most often indictments of deficiency, attributions of fault. This "blame the victim" syndrome leads inevitably to a shrugging off of responsibility by the mainstream and its educational establishment. The problem is "theirs," not "ours." Social and moral judgments are passed down that, in effect, deny children from low-status groups the same access to learning routinely accorded to those from the mainstream.

Operationally, in terms of literacy learning, social and moral judgments based on ignorance of a cultural group most often result in pedagogical decisions and moves that are uninformed, inappropriate, and hence ineffective. From the school's cultural perspective, Donny's problems stemmed from the fact that he was one of those "hillbillies," not from the different schema he had about written language and its purposes and possibilities. His mother's concerns about his progress were not perceived (in the sense of being accorded legitimacy and acted upon) because, according to the prevailing stereotype, she, as an "ignorant river rat," did not know or care about education and was a dysfunctional parent in any case.

The pedagogical moves or—more accurately—*absence* of moves to help Donny and Jenny were thus ineffective; they both failed to learn. This easy acceptance of failure so early in the game[10] would have never happened in a suburban, mainstream school with a child from a mainstream culture. With insider knowledge about middle-class, mainly white, children, school officials would immediately attend to ways in which the school could meet the concerns of the parent and the needs of the child. The stereotypes, expectations, and assumptions about learners from low-status cultures blind educators to possibilities and solutions to the difficulties experienced by so many children in learning to read and write.

Through an interplay of relationships between the culture of low literacy and the effects of low-status cultural membership on educational access, therefore, the literacy attainments historically connected to social class continue in self-perpetuating ways. I believe we are ready to break this cycle. We are at a moment in history where we are again reexamining our educational institutions and practices. The needs of minorities and lower-class citizens are more apparent than they have been for a long time. We are ready, at least on some levels, to reinvent our schools to achieve higher levels of attainment for all of our children.

Schools as Institutions for Learning

If there is no learning occurring in a classroom, can you assume that there is teaching? Admittedly, this conundrum is a variation of the "If a tree falls in a forest. . ." puzzle. It holds, though, in getting at a truth I have sensed both as a teacher and as a teacher of teachers. Teaching and learning reflect different aspects of one act, which is transactional in nature. As such, to deny one must be to deny the other.

This statement may sound unduly harsh to many who truly believe that they are teaching their hearts out in spite of the failure of their students to learn. And I do not mean to denigrate the efforts of all the teachers who struggle to help children learn to read and write in our schools today. Many instructors are succeeding against tremendous odds. However, taken on its own terms, I do believe that my riddle suggests a reality: if even one child does not learn what we believe we have taught, then we have not learned how to teach that child. The responsibility rests, ethically and pragmatically, on the shoulders of educators. This does not mean we are ill-intentioned or bad people, if we fail. It does mean that we have not succeeded; we have not taught.

Schools must become places for learning—for all learners. We can no longer afford the luxury of designing curriculums and educational programs at which only a favored segment of our society can succeed. This does not mean that educational outcome goals need to be lowered or that curriculums need to be "watered down," two simplistic implications feared by some. On the contrary, we need to raise our expectations of outcomes. We must begin to design programs whose aim is to allow learners like Donny and Jenny and other children and adults from minority, low-income, and low-literate homes to learn and to become fully literate. Our curriculums and educational plans must allow access to literacy for every single learner, regardless of social class, minority status, parental education, or home circumstances.

But surely, many may argue, this is the present intention of educational policymakers and practitioners. Perhaps. Yes, as far as lip service and rhetoric are concerned. But anyone working in real schools in actual cities and rural areas knows that the intention does not lead to the accomplishment. After decades of federally funded programs such as Head Start and Chapter One, we still find the same level of social class difference in literacy attainment. We still see millions of illiterate adults[11] and millions more low-literate adults attempting to survive in an increasingly hostile economic environment and raising children in low-literate homes—children who, themselves, will one day perpetuate the dismal cycle.

James Gee, whose work so well captures the essence of the case study of Jenny and Donny, claims that unless one is born into a Discourse community and enjoys the fruits of a full apprenticeship in the Discourse, one cannot ever "be let into the game . . . and be expected to have a fair shot at playing it."[12] The only solution is to change the social order, he claims. His point may be valid, but, in the meantime, teachers must reject this invitation to wait for the millennium. I do not believe that anyone who undertakes to engage in the teaching/learning transaction with learners has the right to assume the failure of any student.

Rather, I am persuaded by the arguments of the scholar Lisa Delpit,[13] who worries that stances like Gee's suggest Discourse determinism, wherein one is locked into one's social class status by one's Discourse. Delpit's arguments include the many personal experiences by minorities who have acquired a secondary Discourse to supplement their primary one and have succeeded in the professional mainstream. All of these people attribute their success directly to *teachers* who *taught* them what they *learned.* These teachers clearly and explicitly taught, according to Delpit, both the "superficial features" of middle-class discourse and the more subtle ones that so often mark class differences.

The problems of poverty and low educational achievement are multidimensional and complex in their relationships. Hunger, inadequate housing, and unpredictable environments all contribute to the schooling problems of children from low-income, minority communities and must be dealt with. We must, however, regard schools as places where children will learn, and learn at rates equal across classes, despite their home circumstances. To accomplish this, we must change in two basic areas.

First, we must recruit and train teachers who know, accept, and celebrate the cultures from which their children come. And this must go beyond the yearly Appalachian Arts celebration or Black History month. Teachers must be given lenses through which they can see all children as learners, with unlimited potential.

These lenses can only be obtained through either an insider's understanding of a particular culture or through directed, thorough education and training in the cultural aspects of the different communities into which our schoolchildren are born and nurtured—the communities that shape the self-identity and world perspectives of all children. The minority educational success stories—the Black Panthers' schools of the 1960s, Marva Collins's school(s) for inner-city children, the many individual accounts from African Americans taught by dedicated African American teachers—must be taken seriously and studied for the truths they can teach us. All of these cases reflect the power of teachers who, as cultural insiders, knew that their students could learn and set about helping them do just that. All children from all sociocultural minority groups, including poor whites, deserve such teachers. With culturally sensitive, culturally knowledgeable lenses in place, teachers, administrators, and policymakers will no longer be so prone to the "blame the victim" syndrome. They will be much more likely to assume responsibility for the educational progress of all children.[14]

The second area in which we must change is the way in which we train and treat our teachers. Assuming a professional responsibility to teach all children requires a proactive stance toward teaching. In the United States, we have eroded this aspect of classroom teaching until only the most strong and individualistic personalities can maintain it.

Proactive teachers are in charge of the learning environment for each child. They enter the classroom armed with a great deal of knowledge about emotional and cognitive development and the elements involved in learning the varied skills and strategies needed for progress toward educational achievement. They know children, and they know how they learn. They know the ways in which children differ and the ways in which they are similar. They know how to nudge, to soothe, to challenge, to reinforce. They know where they are going—the goal—and they are capable of both assessing each child's progress along the way to that goal and taking informed action to prevent each child from straying off of the path.

Proactive teachers do not simply wring their hands when confronted with failure to learn. They do not simply shake their heads and refer unsuccessful children out to "specialists." They do not simply blame the children, themselves, for failure. Nor do they simply blame the children's parents or cultures. Acknowledging complexity, proactive teachers *do* something for each child; they take action based on their knowledge of culture, cognition, and schooling.

Insofar as literacy learning is concerned, an element crucial to a teacher's knowledge base is the role that specific experience with and knowledge about written language plays in the process. This information is still not widely known or appreciated at the classroom level. Donny and Jenny's case provides a clear illustration of this role because Donny's lack of experience with and Jenny's nonuse of print were so stark. Even so, none of Donny's or Jenny's teachers understood the implications of their nonuse of print for their development as literacy learners. More difficult to perceive and appreciate, though, are the many more cases of children who come to school with knowledges about written language that are restricted or different from that expected in formal education.

To allow access to literacy for all children, instruction must recognize and appreciate what the child knows and does not know about print in all dimensions. This is not a judgment of deficiency. This is a diagnostic assessment of what needs to be learned, a determination about where we go from here. Instruction must proceed from that point so that it makes sense to the learner. Anything else is nonsense, both to the learner and to the system that perpetuates it.

For literacy instruction, which is in essence language instruction, to make sense on an individual basis, it must begin with each learner's language and the learner's world that is encoded by that language. It must begin from the learner's primary Discourse. From that point, a knowledgeable, proactive teacher will move the learner along to other worlds, other Discourses. This means that teachers must know and affirm the language and language knowledge of the different learners in the classroom as well as the cultures through which the learners have acquired their language abilities. Teachers, and the school systems within which they operate, cannot be allowed to use children's language as a wall to exclude them from literacy.

Standardized curriculums with their prefocused "scopes and sequences" will not do the trick. Experienced, effective teachers already know this and do their best to "supplement" and vary as needed. The culture of schools seems to be such, however, that teachers are being increasingly locked into instructional practice dictated by administrators and policy boards, by decision makers who are not in the classroom interacting with the Donnys on a moment-to-moment basis. Policies such as "whole class" teaching from only one prepublished curriculum tie teachers' hands and force them to watch helplessly as individual learners like Donny get left behind at the station. The moral quandary into which this throws teachers is wrenching and inexcusable.

If we are to own up to our commitment to equal access to educational opportunity regardless of race, ethnicity, or class, we must arm teachers with knowledge and cultural appreciation and then give them the autonomy, authority, and freedom to teach—each and every child.

Family Literacy

We can work on the issue of low literacy achievement from another perspective as well. The other side of this complex coin involves the capital with which different children arrive at school. The "rich get richer and the poor get poorer" maxim was never so true as when used to describe the educational possibilities of children from well-educated, highly literate homes as compared with equally bright and promising children from homes with no books, low levels of literacy use, and parents unable to or unaware of how they can support their children's schooling.

One day in a public library of a small New England town, I watched a young father hold his two-year-old daughter on his lap as he used a computer to search for a book reference. Surrounded by books and by people reading and writing, this child sat entranced, watching the screen full of print as her daddy read aloud, interspersing comments regarding his task and the process. She sat enfolded in his arms as he paused to write on a piece of paper within her reach whenever he found a reference to his liking. With only this brief encounter, we can predict with a high level of certainty the literacy events and objects surrounding her at home. How lucky she is compared with Donny and Timmy, who had to learn about libraries on a field trip, a trip to a world foreign to them in so many ways.

When this child begins kindergarten, she will bring with her a rich knowledge of the world of print. She will move easily into literacy as she takes from the curriculum the few remaining pieces of information she needs to read and write on her own. As she does this, she will join her parents, relatives, and other members of her culture as a fully literate person, navigating a literate world. When she takes the ubiquitous standardized achievement tests, she will score well above average, as will most other children in her affluent community. Her grades will reflect success. She will be a "good student" in the eyes of her teachers and her parents.

In another school in another community, another five-year-old child will begin kindergarten on the same day. She will have spent her first five years similarly surrounded by loving parents, family, and members of her community. Never having heard a book read aloud or seen anyone of importance do much reading or writing, the school's written stories, alphabet letters, books, and paper and pencil will seem new, strange, and unfamiliar. She will not quickly become an independent reader and writer. In fact, the only place where she "practices" reading and writing will be in school or on homework sheets. Adults in her world may want her to do well in school, but their support will be minimal and at the expense of activities preferable to people in her community. When she and her peers take the achievement tests, they will score well below average. Only the rare few will receive scores "at grade level."

The children who begin school with full, or nearly full, literacy pocketbooks, in terms of the dominant literate Discourse, will consistently and inevitably outperform, outlearn, and outscore those children who arrive at the school door with considerably less. While it is the responsibility of the schools to teach what is needed, programs that focus on increasing the level and degree of literacy in the homes of children have begun and are desperately needed.

Family literacy programs recognize the importance of the home and the community as places of learning. The impetus for these programs comes primarily from the adult education community. Operating under different names and from different funding sources, these programs vary in their approach. Some focus on improving the literacy levels of parents and providing them with parenting tips and literacy activities they can engage in with their children at home. Other programs involve both parents and children in literacy lessons, either separately, together, or in a variation of both.

Policymakers, practitioners, and researchers are just beginning to explore the possibilities of family literacy efforts. The problems of low literacy as they interact with those of poverty and low status are immense and complex. If family literacy programs are to produce significant change, they must be informed by insights that include the many ways that literacy is a cultural practice. Simply applying old, worn-out "methods" of teaching reading and writing as decontextualized skills that emanate from a mainstream perspective to adults and children in settings outside of schools will not work. Placing workbooks and letter-name cards in homes will not move literacy into the lives of people.

Program participants must be allowed access to print through their own perspectives and needs.[15] Literacy must move into the homes of children in natural and meaningful ways. In order to fill their literacy pocketbooks, young children need to experience community members using print to get things done, to learn about and experience the world, and to expand their own human potential.

How this is to be done is still unknown. That it must be done is crucial. We can no longer accept the cruel disparity with which we send children to school and then bemoan the fact that our "lower classes" cannot succeed. Donny and Timmy deserve more. So will their children.

Appendix
Notes
References
Index

Appendix: Research Procedures and Stances

I collected data for this report over a two-year period during which Jenny and Donny worked with me in the Literacy Center, at their home, and in the community as I shared daily errands with them. My stance was that of teacher and researcher. One of my first decisions was, for ethical reasons, to place my role of teacher above that of researcher. Primarily, this meant that I focused on the task of teaching Donny and Jenny how to read and write. Any tests I gave, formal or informal, and any instructional choices I made were decided upon with this goal in mind. This sometimes meant that I did not gather information that would inform the research at all or at the appropriate time if I felt that the act of obtaining the data would hinder Jenny's or Donny's progress. Giving priority to my role as teacher also meant, though, that the outcomes of the study were less influenced by researcher biases than might have been the case. I made a conscious effort not to guide the instruction or the assessment of its success by what I wanted the research to show. Nevertheless, I acknowledge that no research is free of bias. Even the very questions one asks and the data one perceives as significant are driven by theoretical perspectives.

I have discussed my theoretical frame in the Introduction. Within this sociocultural frame, I adopted the following guiding questions suggested by Bernardo Ferdman as crucial to literacy research which acknowledges that the process of becoming literate is mediated by cultural identity:[1]

1. How is literacy defined in the individual's group, and what is its significance? What behaviors are included in this definition?
2. What significance do particular texts have for the individual's cultural identity?
3. How do the particular pedagogical approach, the texts that are used, and the purpose of literacy as communicated by the school relate to the learner's motives and sense of identity (and more subtly, what messages does a reading and writing curriculum communicate about the value of the learner's culture)?
4. What relationship does the learner perceive between the tasks assigned in school and his or her cultural identity? Must the learner change the nature of his or her self-concept in order to do what is asked?

I used various methods to minimize bias and strengthen the validity of the findings.

Teacher

As a teacher, I assumed a clinician role, one that was appropriate to the context of the Literacy Center. As such I attempted to assess, through a variety of measures, what Jenny and Donny, respectively, knew about reading and writing. I used this knowledge to guide my instruction.

The diagnosis and instruction stressed in the Literacy Center is holistic and reflects a view of literacy acquisition that is grounded in psycholinguistic and sociolinguistic research.[2] In essence, this means that learners are encouraged to read and write authentic texts for authentic reasons. In the process of doing so, they are assisted by their teachers in gaining control over the various strategies needed to read and write written discourse. Reading and writing are taught not through a succession of isolated skill work but, rather, in the context of the actual reading and writing of real texts. This means that the majority of the material available for instruction consists of literature, both fiction and nonfiction, reference materials, journals, stationery, and other materials for writing. Separate material for the teaching and learning of phonic skills is also available for teacher reference and occasional selective use with students. Phonic skill is also taught incidentally during the reading and writing activities. Assessment is both informal and formal. Standardized achievement tests are given to provide practice for the graduate students and to place the students on a national norm.

Assessment for instruction is accomplished through informal measures such as informal reading inventories and skilled teacher observation during reading and writing events. A recursive relationship exists between diagnosis and instruction in the Literacy Center. As students respond to instructional moves by their teachers, careful note is taken of areas of difficulty, ease, frustration, or confusion. These observations form the basis of future instruction as well as documentation of the nature of the difficulty.[3] Thus my initial observations of Jenny's and Donny's level of skill and the nature of their problems prompted me to choose particular types of activities for them. As they participated in these activities, I made further observations. Based on what I saw them doing during these activities, I built on and refined my diagnosis of their difficulties. I then initiated further activities, based on the evolving diagnosis.

Researcher

Procedures. My researcher role followed that of my teacher role. I audiotaped virtually every teaching session. I also made field notes of each contact I had with Jenny or Donny. The transcripts of the taped sessions were merged with the field notes for analysis. I visited Donny's classrooms each year, observing him and interviewing his teachers. I recorded these observations and interviews in field note form. I was unable to visit any of Jenny's adult school classes. I did not think it appropriate to request this until the very end of the study. At that time, I scheduled an appointment but was forced to cancel when Jenny became ill. I did have access, however, to Jenny's experiences in her adult school courses through her willingness to share with me the materials and assignments she was given. She always carefully described the nature of the work, whether tutorial or small group, and discussed which activities she felt were helpful and which were not.

I collected as many artifacts as possible from the sessions. Either actual journals or "published" books written by Donny and Jenny, or copies of them, were added to the data. At times this work was taken home by Donny or Jenny for sharing and reading practice before I could copy it. I also gathered samples of reading and writing work from their respective schools.

As I gained the trust of Jenny and Donny, I was invited into their home and lives both as a teacher and as a friend. Appalachians, in general, are noted for their suspicion of outsiders, and, for this reason, research in this community and culture has been difficult and rather scant.[4] Therefore, I chose to wait for an invitation into their home rather than requesting one. I clearly needed to observe in their home if I was to explore the relationship between the nonliteracy of the parents and that of the children. However, I did not wish to violate their sense of privacy or to contribute in any way to a feeling of exploitation by the outside world. The invitation came when Jenny's car failed two months into the study, and she asked me if I would work with Donny at home. Thus began a series of home visits, mainly devoted to teaching. During these visits, I also observed the environment and chatted with Jenny. I met Big Donny a few times and talked briefly with him. These home sessions always included interaction with Timmy, as he was a lively, curious child who found it hard to leave Donny and me to our work.

In addition to the teacher/researcher stance, at times I also assumed the role of participant observer. In the spring of the first year of the study, Jenny asked me to accompany her to an educational supply store so that she could buy some alphabet cards for Timmy. This store was one I had mentioned when she asked about some of the materials in the Literacy Center. I agreed to go, and this began a series of excursions with her into the community for various day-to-day purposes such as grocery shopping and bill paying. During these events I was particularly attentive to the uses and non-uses of print in the environment by Jenny and the children. In addition, Jenny often used these occasions for more intimate, in-depth talk about her life and that of her family. This information was also noted to provide the context for the focus on literacy. I always wrote up field notes immediately after these events.

At the close of the first year, I asked Jenny if I might also visit her home over the summer to observe Donny in his home environment without the overlay of a teaching/learning session (I made other summer home visits specifically for teaching). Although she found it hard to comprehend why anyone would want to do this, she agreed, and I did visit several times to document the home environment and activities and to check on evolving hypotheses regarding home literacy. Again, I wrote up field notes immediately after the event. During all of the participant observer visits and excursions, I refrained from taking notes or audiotaping in order to minimize the self-consciousness of the family.

The study ended after two years. I had accepted a position at another university that entailed my moving out of state. While I did not believe that my work as a teacher with Jenny and Donny was over, I did believe that the research aspect of it was. At my recommendation, Donny continued with the Literacy Center the following year. Just before I moved, I conducted a structured interview with Jenny, asking questions that had not been answered during the course of the study and confirming information I had gleaned from the analysis to that point. Data collection continued, though, for a few months more. Jenny, who at the start of the study could neither read nor write more than a few isolated words, answered my letter to her from my new home with one of her own. I included this initial letter in the analysis. We continue to correspond to this day.

Analysis. The recursive nature of data gathering and analysis required by ethnographic research was evident during the study as I focused and refocused in my attempt to uncover factors surrounding the family's nonliteracy.[5] As mentioned earlier, the original focus was on the relationship between the parents' non-literacy and that of their son. Thus cognitive and psycholinguistic principles tended to inform the sense I made of the information I was gathering. Field notes were reviewed periodically for patterns and themes. Subsequently, I would often ask questions of Jenny or engage Donny in particular tasks to confirm tentative conclusions I had reached or to answer questions that had emerged from the ongoing analysis.

As the study progressed and Donny and Jenny's patterns of success and/or failure became visible, my focus expanded to include issues of minority status and access to literacy. The focus "expanded," rather than "shifted," because my analysis of the data continued to inform me that Donny and Jenny's difficulties with learning to read and write did not result from singular factors such as poverty, minority status, or lack of previous experience with written language. Not one of these factors, by itself, explained the nonliteracy. Rather, a complex interplay of all of them emerged as worthy of attention. As the focus expanded, social and cultural factors were added to the lenses through which I made sense of the data.

The analysis progressed to two sets of final codes as patterns and themes were confirmed. Context, actors, behaviors, and beliefs of the participants were coded in the first set. From this, the data was categorized by major themes. A map of family relationships and literacy histories was drawn to aid in the analysis. I contacted Jenny by letter or phone repeatedly toward the end of the analysis period to confirm my emerging interpretations and to provide missing information.

Midway through the year following the study, after I had moved and had begun the final analysis, I visited the city of Cincinnati, Ohio, to study at the Urban Appalachian Library, a singular repository of research and information about the urban Appalachian population. I also interviewed staff members at the library and urban Appalachian community leaders and activists. In addition, I returned to Jenny's city to visit with Jenny and Donny in their home and observe both Donny and Timmy in their new classrooms (Timmy had started kindergarten). I also observed Donny in the Literacy Center. I interviewed their teachers briefly to gain their perspectives of the boys' success at learning within their respective classrooms. Finally, I observed Jenny, Donny, and Timmy reading and writing within both school and home contexts.

The final analysis is provided in this book. Although the interpretation of the data and the resulting implications for education practice and policy are mine, the voices are to a large degree Jenny's and Donny's. I have chosen to present their voices as I heard them because my sense of the "truth of situation" resides in these voices. I do so, however, with some trepidation. One characteristic of unassimilated urban Appalachians is their retention of certain language patterns and usage. Other groups often use these language patterns to stereotype and make fun of the "hillbillies," a discriminatory practice that is painfully suffered by Appalachians and urban Appalachians nationwide. Jenny, herself, claimed that "my words don't come out the way they're suppose to. That's the way I was brought up."

From the beginning of our association, I enjoyed and perceived Jenny's "words" as part and parcel of the many qualities I admired in her: her ability to cut to the quick of any situation, often reducing bureaucratic pronouncements to nuggets of nonsense; her absolute honesty and straightforward way of living and relating to people; her endearing self-deprecating humor; and her strength and grace as she dealt with one setback after another in her attempts to provide for her family.

Thus, when telling her story, I use her words out of respect for her; her language is integral to her self. A great deal of the power of her story lies in her language. These Appalachian voices and words have been used for so long by bigots and ethnocentrists for mockery and depreciation, however, that it is possible that my use of them will be interpreted as another example of such. This usage is the opposite of my intent. I urge the reader to move beyond society's middle-class bias against this ancient American dialect to the core of truth contained in Jenny's words.

Notes

Introduction

1. I owe a great deal of my thinking on this topic to the work of Lois Weis (1988), whose description of "nested cultural contexts" allowed me to make explicit my implicit understandings of individual learners.

2. Although many perspectives on reading as a social/cultural process have informed my thinking, the frame presented here is most directly derived from the work of Judith Green (1990; Green and Harker, 1988; Green, Harker, and Golden, 1987; Green and Weade, 1986) and David Bloome (Bloome 1983, 1986, 1988; Bloome and Green, 1982). For a broad spectrum of approaches that situate literacy within social/cultural practice, see Cochran-Smith (1984); Cook-Gumperz (1986); Erickson and Schultz (1981); Ferdman (1990); Heath (1983); Ogbu (1974, 1978); and Szwed (1988).

3. See Teale and Sulzby (1986) for an introduction and overview of the emergent literacy perspective and evolving research.

4. The concept of "nested contexts" is used by Lois Weis (1988) to describe the ways in which factors such as social class, gender, and race interconnect and influence each other. Weis argues for greater flexibility in the ways academics treat cate-

gories like social class and race. In the real world, according to Weis, people construct their realities out the interactions of these categories. If we are to promote social justice in the real world, she asserts, we must seek to reflect people's lived experiences rather than attempt to fit them into ad hoc constructions created by academics. For this project, I conceptualized Jenny and her family as contextualized by the nested contexts of illiteracy, social class, and low-caste minority (and, to a degree, gender) status. It is the confluence, interaction, and transactions of these factors that has shaped their lives.

5. I use the term *Discourse* with a capital "D" in the same sense as does James Gee, whose insights on literacy and language capture much of the way in which I thought about the meanings of the data of this study. Gee defines *Discourses* as "ways of being in the world; they are forms of life which integrate words, acts, values, beliefs, attitudes, and social identities as well as gestures, glances, body position, and clothes" (1989, p. 7). The term *discourse* with a small "d," explains Gee, refers to connected pieces of language, and *discourse* is a part of *Discourse.*

2. Jenny and Donny's World

1. This description of the population known as "urban Appalachians" rests on a synthesis of writings (see References), many of which are available only through the Urban Appalachian Library run by the Urban Appalachian Council in Cincinnati, Ohio. Writing in the *Harvard Educational Review,* Maureen Sullivan and Danny Miller (1990) describe the UAC as the primary organization serving urban Appalachian people in Cincinnati. It has served to provide a base for organizing Appalachian migrants and their descendants and to develop model programs to demonstrate effective service delivery and educational methods. In addition, the council library serves as a repository of research and publications documenting and describing the circumstances of urban Appalachians.

2. P. J. Obermiller and M. E. Maloney, "Looking for Appalachians in Pittsburgh: Seeking Deliverance, Finding the Deer Hunter," chap. 2 (p. 13) in Borman and Obermiller (1993).

3. See Borman and Obermiller (1993) and Miller (1978).

4. Borman and Obermiller (1993), chap. 2, pp. 15–16.

5. P. J. Obermiller and M. E. Maloney, "The Current Status and Future Prospects of Urban Appalachians," chap. 1 in Borman and Obermiller (1993).

6. P. J. Obermiller and M. E. Maloney, "From SAMS to Urban Appalachians," in Borman and Obermiller (1993).

7. Obermiller and Maloney (in Borman and Obermiller, 1993, chap. 1) point out that many of the characteristics associated with the group referred to as "urban Appalachian"—and to which I direct attention—have been true primarily for only the first two generations of migrants. The third and fourth generations are better educated, healthier, and less inclined to claim the mountain regions as "home" over the city. Jenny and Big Donny were first-generation migrants and their children, second. Here I highlight the experiences of their cultural group.

8. Giffin (1978), pp. 145–152.

9. Borman and Obermiller (1993), chap. 1, p. 9.

10. Fowler (1978).

11. Giffin (1978), p. 9.

12. C. B. McCoy and V. M. Watkins, "Stereotypes of Appalachian Migrants," in Philliber and McCoy (1981), p. 21.

13. Ibid., p. 22.

14. Ibid.

15. Ibid.

16. Borman and Obermiller (1993), chap. 1.

17. Giffin (1978).

18. For background on the history of social action in the cities as it relates to both African Americans and urban Appalachians, see Tucker (1989).

19. E. M. Penn, K. M. Borman, and F. Hoeweller, "Echoes from the Hill: Urban Appalachian Youths and Educational Reform," chap. 10 in Borman and Obermiller (1993).

20. Ibid.

21. Purcell-Gates and Dahl (1991).

22. Benjamin, Graham, and Phillips (1978). On file at the Urban Appalachian Library, Cincinnati, Ohio.

23. Ibid.

24. Starnes (1990).

3. A World without Print

1. See Clay (1975) for a fascinating account of this phenomenon.

2. Many sources are available on the process of child language acquisition. The following are preliminary suggestions: R. Brown (1973); Ferguson and Slobin (1973); Gleason (1993); and Snow and Ferguson (1977).

3. This claim seemed too all-encompassing to me. Beginning reading/writing teachers recognize that children come to school with different levels of knowledge and different abilities to succeed in beginning literacy instruction. In undertaking this research I believed that it was important to examine the ways in which these differing levels of background knowledge both developed before the school years and affected the ways in which children "learn" in school.

4. Within the scope of this book I cannot fully describe the many complexities and issues that exist in the study of oral and written language relationships and differences. For those who wish to explore this issue more deeply and broadly, see Chafe and Danielewicz (1986) for more detail on the featural differences between oral and written discourse, including discussions of pragmatic factors that motivate these differences. See also Horowitz and Samuels (1986), A. Rubin (1978), and D. Rubin (1987).

5. The transcription conventions used here include (a) conventional, written, punctuation marks indicate sentence-final fall intonation(.), fall-rise intonation(,), and rising-question intonation (?); (b) dots between intonation units indicate relative

pause length; (c) question marks between slashes mean the words could not be distinguished on the tape; (d) the appearance of language for Speaker 1 and for Speaker 2 on the same line means their speech is overlapping; nonoverlapping speech appears on subsequent, alternating lines to indicate turn-taking.

6. Chafe and Danielewicz (1986) suggest that processing demands influence the different forms that oral and written forms take. For example, they posit that the relatively short "intonation units" that make up the basic unit of speech "fits" the listener's short-term memory capacity (five units, plus or minus two) on which the oral processing of speech depends.

7. As Chafe and Danielewicz (1986) point out, oral language can take many different forms, as can written language. The context of the language use, the speaker's or writer's purpose, and the subject matter can all influence the forms taken by language. "Aspects of written style may be borrowed by speakers when it suits them, just as aspects of spoken style may be borrowed by writers" (p. 84).

8. To describe written language as "decontextualized" can be misleading if one extends the meaning of this term beyond "shared physical context." I use the term "recontextualized" to indicate the ways in which a writer presents information so that the physical, or mental, context can be retrieved from the written text alone; the content is recontextualized within the written text. See Purcell-Gates (1991) for a description of the ways in which young, preliterate children can do this if they have had a vast amount of experience with written text through being read to.

9. I discuss this conceptualization of emergent literacy research more fully in Purcell-Gates (1986).

10. See Taylor (1985), entitled *Family Literacy: Young Children Learning to Read and Write*. Subsequent to this book, which included only children of middle-class families, Denny Taylor worked with Catherine Dorsey-Gaines (Taylor and Dorsey-Gaines, 1988) to study the ways in which literacy also perme-

ates the lives of many low socioeconomic status minority children. The children and families in this latter study differed from Jenny's family in that literacy played important roles in their daily lives, and the children were relatively successful in school.

11. Harste, Woodward, and Burke (1984) also describe in *Language Stories and Literacy Lessons* how children who have experienced print in their lives grasp its semiotic nature as an essential early concept. They implicitly "know" that print "says" something; that it codes meaning linguistically.

12. Sulzby (1985).

13. The data from this study produced several different analyses, all of which revealed different aspects of the ways in which young, well-read-to children, who were not yet reading independently, had grasped and implicitly mastered the decontextualized, syntactically complex and lexically sophisticated nature of written narrative as compared to oral, personal narrative. See Purcell-Gates (1988), (1991), and (1992) for complete reports of these analyses and relevant discussions of the import of the results.

14. See Purcell-Gates (1994) for evidence that a significant correlation exists between young children's scores on a test of knowledge of the alphabetic principle and the degree to which their parents read to them (measured by frequency of storybook reading events per hour observed).

4. Becoming Literate

1. Considerable acrimonious debate is currently raging in the reading field over the relative value of skills-based instruction versus what has become known as "whole language" or "literature-based" reading instruction. While I do not go into the details of this debate here, it is important for the reader to understand that the skills-based instruction I refer to in this study is most commonly incarnated as reading instruction dictated by a basal reading series with a preconceived scope and sequence of "skills" and "subskills" that teachers are to teach

to their students as described in the accompanying teacher's manual (Goodman et al., 1987a). Materials used in basal reading series include workbooks or work sheets for practice on the skills being taught, books or "readers" containing reading selections for the learners to practice their skills, and, often, publisher-designed assessments to measure mastery of the pre-sequenced skills. Basal series also usually include supplementary materials for "extension" activities.

2. Chall (1983).

3. Jenny's total years of school include grades 1–7 and over three years of fairly regular attendance at adult basic education classes.

4. Readers familiar with the field of learning disabilities may wonder why Donny, and possibly Jenny, were not tested and diagnosed as dyslexic and assigned to special classes for instruction. This question raises several issues relative to this study. First, the designation of learners as learning disabled varies across school districts and is contingent to a great degree upon local standards and achievement levels (see Bryant and McLoughlin, 1972, and Myers and Hammill, 1990, for an indepth discussion). Donny and Jenny were both students in an urban district with overall lower levels of achievement than those of the surrounding suburban areas. Thus, I speculate, their lack of progress did not stand out as much as it would in another district. In addition, their "urban Appalachian" status would have made their lack of progress seem more "normal" than the same profile observed in a white child not identifiable as a member of this minority. The second issue relates to the identification of a learning disability. The definition accepted by the National Joint Committee on Learning Disabilities (1989) defines learning disabilities as "a general term that refers to a heterogeneous group of disorders manifested by significant difficulties in the acquisition and use of listening, speaking, reading, writing, reasoning, or mathematical abilities. These disorders are intrinsic to the individual, presumed to be due to central nervous system dysfunction, and may occur across the life span.

Problems in self-regulatory behaviors, social perception, and social interaction may exist with learning disabilities but do not by themselves constitute a learning disability. Although learning disabilities may occur concomitantly with other handicapping conditions (for example, sensory impairment, mental retardation, serious emotional disturbance) or with extrinsic influences (such as cultural differences, insufficient or inappropriate instruction), they are not the result of those conditions or influences" (p. 1). For Donny, at least, extrinsic factors, specifically lack of exposure to written language, seemed the stronger of the explanations for his lack of progress at the time I first met him. As time went on, and Jenny and Donny both learned the skills and strategies needed for reading and writing through instruction adapted to fit this original hypothesis, the diagnosis of dyslexia became even less appropriate. The entire area of the etiology of reading/writing "disorders" is complex and less than clear. The bottom line, regardless of one's comfort with specific diagnoses is, I believe, that instruction must lead to progress for individual children. If it does not, then the instruction must adapt until it does.

5. The theory embodied in the instruction in the Literacy Center owes a great deal to the work of Kenneth S. Goodman. His original work with miscue analysis brought the discipline of psycholinguistics directly into the study of reading process and, later, reading instruction. See Goodman (1970, 1986) for descriptions of his perspectives on literacy, language, and thought and its implications for literacy instruction.

6. Rhodes and Dudley-Marling (1988), p. 17.

7. See Clarke (1988).

8. The exception to this would be those readers who are "dysphonetic" in that, for neurological reasons, they are unable to hear and distinguish the phonemic base of written English.

9. See Adams (1990) for a thorough synthesis of the research of phonemic awareness and learning to read.

10. I possessed a great deal of knowledge about the curriculum of this particular school district due to (1) my membership

on a national committee to review its reading/writing curriculum and (2) the recent completion of a study during which I had observed in kindergarten and first-grade classrooms during reading/writing instruction for two years.

11. Sendak (1963).

12. The partner-reading procedure is often helpful when developing readers are reading text that is at the upper limit of their ability. The teacher, or "partner," reads the text alternately with the student, according to agreed-upon divisions of labor, for example, alternate paragraphs, alternate pages, and so on. By providing this support, the teacher helps to maintain the reader's focus and interest in the text as well as providing him/her with contextualized opportunities to hear word pronunciations, sentence intonations, and syntactical phrasings.

13. Learners can build relevant linguistic knowledge about written language from *hearing* it as it is read to them. See my study (Purcell-Gates, 1988) of well-read-to kindergartners, which shows the degree to which these prereaders "knew" the vocabulary style, syntactic style, and "decontextualized" ways of saying inherent in written narrative. I hypothesize that the same process of learning holds true for exposition read aloud as well, although this has not been confirmed in quite the same way. I often recommend to parents and teachers that they read aloud to their children/students from texts that are linguistically too difficult for them to read independently. In this way, the adults are constantly providing the cognitive/linguistic foundation upon which the children (at all ages) will draw as they continue to develop as readers and writers.

14. See Rhodes and Dudley-Marling (1988) and Johnston (1992).

15. See Dyson (1982).

16. I am making a point of the need for direct instruction because of the ambivalence expressed in the professional literature, and felt by many teachers, toward the role of such teaching. For several decades now, a model of learning based on developmental principles has been favored by many leading

researchers and theorists. This view advocates classroom instruction that honors and reflects a "natural" developmental progression toward full literacy. The role of direct instruction for this form of learning is unclear to many teachers; some would actively avoid such guidance, feeling that the children should be allowed to discover and sort out for themselves the underlying patterns and rules of print. Others feel that direct instruction should only take the form of answering children's questions at "teachable moments." Much of this debate stems from a paradigm confusion. The aversion to the term "direct instruction" for some practitioners stems from a desire to avoid many of the limitations of practice that moves all children through a preset scope and sequence of isolated skill work regardless of the conceptual development of individual children. I do not interpret direct instruction to mean an all-controlling teacher telling whole classes what to do and when to do it. Nor do I interpret direct instruction to imply the rote, mindless use of work sheets and/or workbooks as reading/writing instruction. Rather, I use the term to describe the clear, unambiguous explanations of underlying rules of written language and how one goes about reading and writing it in the many pragmatic contexts in which it functions.

Unless one assumes that there is something inherently "wrong" with individual learners that affects their learning processes, we have to believe that if they had been able to "figure it out" for themselves, they would have done so earlier. If one is an outsider to a culture, it is not possible to learn the underlying rules and ways of meaning of that culture implicitly. We can test this by thinking of a culture to which we do not belong. Imagine being forced to live in it and being judged on your success as a member. Clear, helpful tips regarding the way in which the culture works would certainly be more helpful than being left to sink or swim.

5. In Her Own Words

1. Clay (1991).

2. This procedure, known most commonly as "language experience," entails not transcribing "speech" (see Chapter 3) but, rather, transcribing the children's oral version of some form of written text. Teachers will typically elicit from a group or an individual a "story." The very act of *writing* the story down (which the teacher, or scribe, does) provides a "written" context of situation for the elicited language. See Purcell-Gates (1989), though, for a discussion of the ways in which we may sometimes confuse children during language experience activities with our directions for "telling about" an event when, in fact, we mean to "write about" an event.

3. Vygotsky (1962).

4. A formal report of this analysis of Jenny's writing has been published in the *Journal of Reading.* See Purcell-Gates (1993).

5. This analysis was based on the description of Appalachian dialect by Wolfram and Christian (1976).

6. To recognize a word "automatically" means to know it as a whole without resort to sounding out or other forms of word analysis. See Samuels (1985) for a description of this process. My statements here should not be taken as advocacy of drill and practice of individual words, indeed, I mean just the opposite as a means of acquiring a large store of automatically recognized words ("sight" words). Individual words must be processed (read/recognized) repeatedly as they occur in text/discourse with all of the attendant functions and properties of language, with the focus on meaning. It was the futile effort by Jenny to memorize *disconnected* words over the years that blocked her progress as a reader and a writer.

6. Print Enters the World of Donny and Jenny

1. Sendak (1963).

7. Who Reads and Writes in My World?

1. Of particular interest to this aspect of emergent literacy

are: Bissex (1980); Clay (1975); Dyson (1989); and Read (1971).

2. Durkin (1966).

3. Taylor (1985).

4. Personal experience and anecdote as well as some recent research has highlighted the class differences in parental stance toward learning about reading and writing through child-directed exploration and play. Heath's (1983) study of middle-class and working-class parents and children suggested that working- and lower-class groups view learning to read and write as the result of didactic teaching and specialized "work" devoted to learning letter names and words and working toward accuracy. Delpit (1986, 1988) suggests a similar lack of fit between the progressive, child-centered model of learning through exploration favored by educated middle-class parents and a more directive, teacher/parent-directed model of learning more familiar to many African Americans. Much more research is called for in this area before we can comfortably say that one model of learning accounts for all children from all cultures.

5. Although Jenny came to believe that she could read and write to a limited extent, she continued to proclaim that she could not whenever she talked about herself. This claim appeared to be habituated and automatic. When I would interrupt to counter her, she would stop, think, and then admit that, well, yes, she could read some things now. The gestalt of her self-image, however, included that of herself as a nonreader for a time considerably beyond her successful move into literacy. Her world was a nonliterate's world, and worlds do not change overnight or with the simple acquisition of some reading and writing ability.

8. Exclusion and Access

1. Anonymous personal account provided by Chester Laine, professor of education and member of the Urban Appalachian Council Advisory Board in Cincinnati, Ohio, in 1988.

2. I do not delve into issues of the impact of literacy on cognition and/or culture here (see Olson, Torrance, and Hildyard, 1985; Scribner and Cole, 1978). I am limiting my discussion to the linguistic differentiation of oral and written discourse and the ways in which written language can influence one's oral language.

3. From Holling (1969).

4. See Chafe and Danielewicz (1986).

9. The Complexities of Culture, Language, Literacy, and Cognition

1. See Kaestle et al. (1991) for a fascinating and comprehensive review of literacy in America since 1880. Kaestle and his colleagues chronicle the literacy gap between the classes over time and conclude, "In spite of the expansion of education and the proliferation of reading materials, literacy remains inextricably tied to the social structure. It reflects chronic differences among groups as well as the distribution of power in our society" (p. 127).

2. The notion that poor whites do not elicit immediate racism because they are not "people of color" needs to be explored. It is true that they are white, as are most members of the middle class and privileged mainstream. I suspect, however, that poor whites are easily recognized as low-caste by their ways of dressing, acting, and speaking.

3. The anthropologist John Ogbu (1974, 1978) theorizes that the failure of "castelike minorities" to achieve academically as well as whites in the United States is due to resistance by members of these minorities to standards and values held by the dominant culture. He claims that minority students equate learning standard English and other academic skills with "acting white" and thus involving a loss of their own social identity and self-worth. Paolo Freire (1970) believes that the liberation of the lower classes worldwide lies in a pedagogy for literacy that is rooted in their own experience and growing

awareness of their oppression and oppressors. Both of these theories are applicable to this study of Jenny and Donny, who have low-caste minority status even though they are "white." Here I have sought to highlight the roles that language and teaching played in this story of nonliteracy contextualized by the reality of lower-class oppression.

4. I owe, along with others in my profession, a profound debt to Shirley Brice Heath (1983) for her ground-breaking research and insights into the different ways in which children from different sociocultural communities learn to use language at home and at school. Heath's work has been instrumental in focusing literacy researchers on the relationships between the cultural uses of language and success in school.

5. Here I am not talking about those learners who have significant difficulty learning to read and/or write due primarily to supposed neurological differences.

6. See Purcell-Gates (1994) and Purcell-Gates and Dahl (1991).

7. Although the overwhelming majority of urban Appalachians are white, with many of Irish, Scottish, and English heritage, African American migrants from the Appalachia region are also included by most demographers and scholars in this cultural group. Their numbers are relatively small, however.

8. Michael Maloney who, along with Ernie Mynatt, was an early activist and advocate for urban Appalachians, discusses in an interview (Tucker, 1989) the difficulties urban Appalachians have had coalescing as a political power to demand their fair share of the social service pie. Contrasting the effort with the success of African Americans, who worked mainly through black churches, Maloney explains, "Appalachian mountain people [are] the most religiously divided ethnic group in the world. We've transplanted all those sects to the city, and it's hard to build community organization around a bunch of sects, most of which teach their people not to work to build community—the kingdom of God on this earth—but to look for the heavenly Jerusalem to come" (p. 44). In addition, Tucker

points out that Appalachians in the city are reluctant to claim membership in a group due to the intense discrimination against their culture.

9. As recently as November of 1992, denigrating references to rural and urban Appalachians appeared on the front page of the "National Report" section of the *New York Times* (November 27, 1992). The reporter Michael Kelly quotes a Bill Clinton supporter from Arkansas, celebrating his presidential victory: "When I moved here, my mother said she didn't even know where Little Rock was. She said there was nothing here but hoedowns and hillbillies. Bill has showed people Arkansas is a real state. Little Rock is a real city, and we're real people" (p. A20). One can only speculate on the feelings of the "hillbillies" who are apparently *not* real people for this lady and many others in mainstream society.

10. In Donny's case. We cannot accurately account for the school's degree of response to Jenny's school failure, although we can speculate.

11. A recent study by the Educational Testing Service and released by the Education Department concluded that "nearly half of the nation's 191 million adult citizens are not proficient enough in English to write a letter about a billing error or to calculate the length of a bus trip from a published schedule" (reported in the *New York Times,* September 9, 1993, by William Celis III).

12. Gee (1989), p. 10.

13. See Delpit (1993).

14. Foster (1990) and King (1993) make similar arguments regarding the need for more African American teachers. King points out that Foster learned through her study of African American teachers that they expect their African American children to learn and "do not rationalize student failure by blaming the family or society" (King, 1993, p. 118).

15. See Auerbach (1989) and Fingeret (1987) for more insights into the need for socioculturally relevant adult education programs.

Appendix

1. Ferdman (1990), pp. 197–198.

2. See Goodman (1970, 1986), Harste (1984), and Smith (1975, 1978, 1985) for more information on psycholinguistic and sociopsycholinguistic theory as it relates to literacy acquisition and development.

3. This description of the policies and procedures of the Literacy Center are valid for the time span (1989–1991) in which the study was conducted.

4. See Wolfram and Christian (1976) for insights into research into Appalachian culture and language.

5. See Dobert (1982), Goetz and LeCompte (1984), and Miles and Huberman (1984) for assumptions and procedures for qualitative and ethnographic research as they relate to data gathering and analysis.

References

Adams, J. 1971. Our Appalachian children face special problems in school. Reprint from the *Cincinnati Post* and *Times Star* on file at UAC Library. Cincinnati, Ohio: Urban Appalachian Council.

Adams, M. J. 1990. *Beginning to read: Thinking and learning about print.* Cambridge, Mass.: MIT Press.

Arnold, E. T. 1990. Al, Abner, and Appalachia. *Appalachian Journal* (Spring): 262–275.

Auerbach, E. R. 1989. Toward a social-contextual approach to family literacy. *Harvard Educational Review,* 59: 159–174.

Ball, S. A. 1975. "Whup 'em good." Paper on file at UAC Library. Cincinnati, Ohio: Urban Appalachian Council.

Benjamin, R., M. Graham, and M. Phillips. 1978. Color them children. Series appearing in the *Cincinnati Post,* beginning July 22. Cincinnati, Ohio.

Bissex, G. 1980. *Gnys at wrk: A child learns to write and read.* Cambridge, Mass.: Harvard University Press.

Bloome, D. 1983. Reading as a social process. In B. A. Hutson, ed., *Advances in reading/language research,* vol. 2, pp. 165–196. Greenwich, Conn.: JAI Press.

——— 1986. *Literacy and schooling.* Norwood, N.J.: Ablex.

——— 1988. *Classrooms and literacy.* Norwood, N.J.: Ablex.

Bloome, D., and J. L. Green. 1982. The social contexts of

reading: A multidisciplinary perspective. In B. A. Hutson, ed., *Advances in reading/language research,* vol. 1. Greenwich, Conn.: JAI Press.

Borman, K. M. 1991. *Overwhelmed in Cincinnati: Urban Appalachian children and youth.* Report to U.S. Department of Education.

Borman, K. M., and P. J. Obermiller, eds. 1993. *From mountain to metropolis: Appalachian migrants in the American city.* New York: Greenwood Press.

Brown, J. S., and H. K. Schwarzweller. 1978. The Appalachian family. In *Perspectives on urban Appalachians: An introduction to mountain life, migration, and urban adaptation, and a guide to the improvement of social services.* Cincinnati, Ohio: Urban Appalachian Council.

Brown, R. 1973. *A first language: The early stages.* Cambridge, Mass.: Harvard University Press.

Bryant, N. D., and J. A. McLoughlin. 1972. Subject variables: Definition, incidence, characteristics, and correlates. In N. D. Bryant and C. E. Kass, eds., *Final report,* vol. 1, *USOE contract, Leadership training institute in learning disabilities,* pp. 5–158. Sponsored by the Department of Special Education, University of Arizona, Tucson, and Program Development Branch, Division of Educational Service, Bureau of Education for the Handicapped, USOE, grant no. OEO-0-71-4425 604, project no. 127145.

Chafe, W., and J. Danielewicz. 1986. Properties of spoken and written language. In R. Horowitz and S. J. Samuels, eds., *Comprehending oral and written language.* New York: Academic Press.

Chall, J. 1983. *Stages of reading development.* New York: McGraw-Hill.

Clarke, L. K. 1988. Invented versus traditional spelling in first graders' writings: Effects on learning to spell and read. *Research in the Teaching of English,* 22: 281–309.

Clay, M. M. 1975. *What did I write?* Auckland, New Zealand: Heinemann.

——— 1991. *Becoming literate: The construction of inner control.* Auckland, New Zealand: Heinemann.

Cochran-Smith, M. 1984. *The making of a reader.* Norwood, N.J.: Ablex.

Comer, J. P. 1988. Educating poor minority children. *Scientific American,* 259: 42–48.

Cook-Gumperz, J. 1986. *The social construction of literacy.* New York: Cambridge University Press.

Delpit, L. D. 1986. Skills and other dilemmas of a progressive black educator. *Harvard Educational Review,* 56: 379–385.

——— 1988. The silenced dialogue: Power and pedagogy in educating other people's children. *Harvard Educational Review,* 59: 280–298.

——— 1993. The politics of teaching literate discourse. In T. Perry and J. W. Fraser, eds., *Freedom's plow: Teaching in the multicultural classroom,* pp. 285–295. New York: Routledge.

Dobert, M. L. 1982. *Ethnographic research: Theory and application for modern schools and societies.* New York: Praeger.

Durkin, D. 1966. *Children who read early.* New York: Teachers College Press.

Dyson, A. 1982. Reading, writing, and language: Young children solving the written language puzzle. *Language Arts,* 59: 204–214.

——— 1989. *Multiple worlds of child writers: Friends learning to write.* New York: Teachers College Press.

Erickson, F., and J. Schultz. 1981. When is a context? In J. Green and C. Wallat, eds., *Ethnography and language in educational settings.* Norwood, N.J.: Ablex.

Fay, J. D. 1977. *Toward understanding the Appalachian child in the urban school.* Paper on file at UAC Library. Cincinnati, Ohio: Urban Appalachian Council.

Ferdman, B. M. 1990. Literacy and cultural identity. *Harvard Educational Review,* 60: 181–204.

Ferguson, C. A., and Slobin, D. I., eds. 1973. *Studies of child language development.* New York: Holt, Rinehart and Winston.

Fingeret, A. 1987. *Directions in ethnographic adult literacy research.*

Paper presented at the Thirty-Second Annual Convention of the International Reading Association. Anaheim, Calif.

Foster, M. 1990. The politics of race: Through the eyes of African-American teachers. *Journal of Education,* 172: 123–141.

Fowler, G. L. 1978. Up here and down home: Appalachians in cities. In *Perspectives on urban Appalachians: An introduction to mountain life, migration, and urban adaptation, and a guide to the improvement of social services.* Cincinnati, Ohio: Urban Appalachian Council.

Freire, P. 1970. *Pedagogy of the oppressed.* New York: Seabury Press.

Gee, J. P. 1989. Literacy, discourse, and linguistics: Introduction. *Journal of Education,* 171: 5–17.

Giffin, R. 1978. From Cinder Hollow to Cincinnati. In *Perspectives on urban Appalachians: An introduction to mountain life, migration, and urban adaptation, and a guide to the improvement of social services.* Cincinnati, Ohio: Urban Appalachian Council.

Gleason, J. B., ed. 1993. *The development of language.* 3d ed. New York: Macmillan.

Goetz, J. P., and M. D. LeCompte. 1984. *Ethnography and qualitative design in educational research.* San Diego, Calif.: Academic Press.

Goodman, K. 1970. Reading: A psycholinguistic guessing game. In H. Singer and R. B. Ruddell, eds., *Theoretical models and processes of reading.* Newark, Del.: International Reading Association.

——— 1986. *What's whole in whole language.* Portsmouth, N.H.: Heinemann.

Goodman, K., P. Shannon, Y. S. Freeman, and S. Murphy. 1987a. *Report card on basal readers.* New York: Richard C. Owen Publishers.

Goodman, K., E. B. Smith, R. Meredith, and Y. M. Goodman. 1987b. *Language and thinking in school.* New York: Richard C. Owen Publishers.

Gosham, T. 1980. The children the schools leave behind. Article appearing in the *Cincinnati Post,* April 19, p. IA. Cincinnati, Ohio.

Green, J. L. 1990. Reading is a social process. In J. Howell, A. McNamara, and M. Clough, eds., *Social context of literacy*, pp. 104–123. Canberra, Australia: ACT Department of Education, Canberra.

Green, J. L., and J. O. Harker. 1988. *Multiple perspective analysis of classroom discourse*. Norwood, N.J.: Ablex.

Green, J. L., J. O. Harker, and J. M. Golden. 1987. Lesson construction: Differing views. In G. Noblitt and W. Pink, eds., *The social context of schooling*. Norwood, N.J.: Ablex.

Green, J. L., and R. Weade. 1986. Exploring "reading in everyday events." In D. Bloome, ed., *Literacy and schooling*. Norwood, N.J.: Ablex.

Harste, J. 1984. Examining our assumptions: A transactional view of literacy and learning. *Research in the Teaching of English*, 18: 84–108.

Harste, J., V. Woodward, and C. Burke. 1984. *Language stories and literacy lessons*. Exeter, N.H.: Heinemann.

Heath, S. B. 1983. *Ways with words*. New York: Cambridge University Press.

Holling, H. C. 1969. *Paddle to the sea*. Boston: Houghton Mifflin.

Horowitz, R., and S. J. Samuels, eds. 1986. *Comprehending oral and written language*. New York: Academic Press.

Johnston, P. H. 1992. *Constructive evaluation of literate activity*. New York: Longman.

Kaestle, C. F., H. Damon-Moore, L. C. Stedman, K. Tinsley, and W. V. Trollinger, Jr. 1991. *Literacy in the United States*. New Haven, Conn.: Yale University Press.

King, S. H. 1993. The limited presence of African American teachers. *Review of Educational Research*, 63: 115–149.

LaBerge, D., and S. J. Samuels. 1974. Toward a theory of automatic information processing in reading. *Cognitive Psychology*, 6: 293–323.

McKee, D. M., and P. J. Obermiller. 1978. The invisible neighborhood: Appalachians in Ohio's cities. In *Perspectives on urban Appalachians: An introduction to mountain life, migration, and urban adaptation, and a guide to the improvement of social services*. Cincinnati, Ohio: Urban Appalachian Council.

Miles, M. B., and A. M. Huberman. 1984. *Qualitative data analysis*. Beverly Hills, Calif.: Sage Publications.

Miller, T. R. 1978. Urban appalachian ethnic identity: The current situation. In *Perspectives on urban Appalachians: An introduction to mountain life, migration, and urban adaptation, and a guide to the improvement of social services.* Cincinnati, Ohio: Urban Appalachian Council.

Myers, P. I., and D. D. Hammill. 1990. *Learning disabilities*. 4th ed. Austin, Tex.: Pro-Ed.

National Joint Committee on Learning Disabilities. 1989. Letter from NJCLD to member organizations. Topic: Modifications to the NJCLD definition of learning disabilities. September 18.

Ogbu, J. 1974. *The next generation: An ethnography of education in an urban neighborhood.* New York: Academic Press.

——— 1978. *Minority education and caste.* New York: Academic Press.

Olson, D. R., N. Torrance, and A. Hildyard, eds. 1985. *Literacy, language, and learning: The nature and consequences of reading and writing.* New York: Cambridge University Press.

Philliber, W. W., and C. B. McCoy, eds., with H. C. Dillingham. 1981. *The invisible minority: Urban Appalachians.* Lexington, Ky.: University Press of Kentucky.

Purcell-Gates, V. 1986. Three levels of understanding about written language acquired by young children prior to formal instruction. In J. Niles and R. Lalik, eds., *Solving problems in literacy: Learners, teachers, and researchers.* Rochester, N.Y.: National Reading Conference.

——— 1988. Lexical and syntactic knowledge of written narrative held by well-read-to kindergartners and second graders. *Research in the Teaching of English,* 22: 128–160.

——— 1989. What research into oral/written language differences can tell us about beginning reading and writing instruction. *Reading Teacher,* 42 (4): 290–295.

——— 1991. Ability of well-read-to kindergartners to decontextualize/recontextualize experience into a written-narrative register. *Language and Education: An International Journal,* 5: 177–188.

——— 1992. Roots of response. *Journal of Narrative and Life History,* 2: 151–161.

——— 1993. I ain't never read my *own* words before. *Journal of Reading,* 37: 210–219.

——— 1994. *Relationships between parental literacy skills and functional uses of print and children's ability to learn literacy skills.* Grant no. X257A20223. Washington, D.C.: National Institute for Literacy.

Purcell-Gates, V., and K. Dahl. 1991. Low-SES children's success and failure at early literacy learning in skills-based classrooms. *JRB: A Journal of Literacy,* 23: 1–34.

Read, C. 1971. Preschool children's knowledge of English phonology. *Harvard Educational Review,* 41: 1–34.

Rhodes, L. K., and C. Dudley-Marling. 1988. *Readers and writers with a difference: A holistic approach to teaching learning disabled and remedial students.* Portsmouth, N.H.: Heinemann.

Rubin, A. D. 1978. *A theoretical taxonomy of the differences between oral and written language.* Technical report no. 335. Champaign, Ill.: Center for the Study of Reading, University of Illinois. January.

Rubin, D. 1987. Divergence and convergence between oral and written communication. *Topics in Language Disorders,* 7: 1–18.

Salstrom, P., D. V. McCauley, H. Dorgan, and A. Waller. 1990. What doth it profit? The study of mountain religion. *Appalachian Journal* (Fall): 56–81.

Samuels, S. J. 1985. Automaticity and beginning reading. In J. Osborn, P. T. Wilson, and R. C. Anderson, eds., *Reading education: Foundations for a literate America,* 215–230. Lexington, Mass.: Lexington Books.

Scribner, S., and M. Cole. 1978. Literacy without schooling: Testing for intellectual effects. *Harvard Educational Review,* 48, 448–461.

Sendak, M. 1963. *Where the wild things are.* New York: Harper & Row.

Smith, F. 1975. The role of prediction in reading. *Elementary Education,* 52: 305–311.

——— 1978. *Understanding reading.* 2nd ed. New York: Holt, Rinehart and Winston.

——— 1985. *Reading.* 2nd ed. London: Cambridge University Press.

Snow, C. E., and C. A. Ferguson, eds. 1977. *Talking to children: Language input and acquisition.* New York: Cambridge University Press.

Starnes, B. 1990. Appalachian students, parents, and culture as viewed by their teachers. *Urban Appalachian Advocate,* January: 1–4.

Sullivan, M., and D. Miller. 1990. Cincinnati's urban Appalachian council and Appalachian identity. *Harvard Educational Review,* 60: 106–124.

Sulzby, E. 1985. Children's emergent abilities to read favorite storybooks: A developmental study. *Reading Research Quarterly,* 20: 458–481.

——— 1990. Writing and reading instruction and assessment for young children: Issues and implications. Paper commissioned by the Forum on the Future of Children and Families of the National Academy of Sciences and the National Association of State Boards of Education.

Szwed, J. F. 1988. The ethnography of literacy. In E. R. Kintgen, B. M. Kroll, and M. Rose, eds., *Perspectives on literacy.* Carbondale, Ill.: Southern Illinois University Press.

Taylor, D. 1985. *Family literacy: Children learning to read and write.* Exeter, N.H.: Heinemann.

Taylor, C., and Dorsey-Gaines, C. 1988. *Growing up literate: Learning from inner city families.* Portsmouth, N.H.: Heinemann.

Teale, W., and Sulzby, E. 1986. *Emergent literacy: Writing and reading.* Norwood, N.J.: Ablex.

Tucker, B. 1989. Interview with Michael Maloney. *Appalachian Journal* (Fall): 34–49.

Vygotsky, L. S. 1962. *Thought and language.* Cambridge, Mass.: Harvard University Press.

Wagner, T. E. 1977. Urban schools and Appalachian children. *Urban Education,* 12: 283–296.

——— 1978. Urban schools and Appalachian children: Old values, new problems, no answers. In *Perspectives on urban Appalachians: An introduction to mountain life, migration, and urban adaptation, and a guide to the improvement of social services.* Cincinnati, Ohio: Urban Appalachian Council.

Weis, L., ed. 1988. *Class, race, and gender in American education.* Albany, N.Y.: State University of New York Press.

Wolfram, W., and D. Christian. 1976. *Appalachian speech.* Arlington, Va.: Center for Applied Linguistics.

Index